Food and Drink Dot Marker Coloring Book for Kids Ages 1–5

Bold and Easy Lines to Color with Fun Weekly Educational Activities | Boost Creativity and Fine Motor Skills for Children Under 5 | Scissor Practice | Maze Puzzles | Toddler & Preschool Counting

POLYMATH
Panda

ISBN: 978-1-953149-78-7

This Book Belongs To:

_____

Grab Your Dot Markers and Dive into 50 Fun-Filled Pages of Ice Cream, Pizza, Burger, and many more!

Featuring a wide variety of Food and Drinks to Color. Includes engaging activities like Cutting, Counting, Mazes, Match the Foods or Drinks, and many more fun activities, all designed with large, easy-to-color dots. Perfectly compatible with all leading dot marker brands with consistent 0.75 inch (18mm) dots.

This book is a fantastic fit for young explorers aged 1 - 5. It's crafted to enhance your child's early learning journey with delightful Food and Drinks designs that connect words, images, and colors. Our team of skilled designers has ensured each page stimulates your child's imagination and helps build their fine motor skills, making learning an exciting adventure!

We understand the enthusiasm of young dot marker artists, so we've designed each page to be single-sided, minimizing the risk of colors bleeding through. Additionally, placing a sheet of paper or card between the pages can be a great way to keep everything tidy!

Thank you for choosing this book! We hope it brings you and your child countless hours of dot marker joy and learning.

Free Printable Activity Book!

- **Ignites Imagination:** Coloring with a story helps kids picture scenes and boost creativity.
- **Boosts Reading:** Following the story while coloring improves reading skills naturally.
- **Enhances Focus:** Storytelling with coloring keeps kids engaged and builds concentration.
- **Fosters Connection:** Coloring helps kids emotionally bond with characters and plots.
- **Fun Learning:** Makes learning enjoyable and easy through playful coloring.

QR Code in the Back of the Book

Enjoying this Book?

We'd love to hear your thoughts

We may just send
you something special.

Week 1

Ice Cream

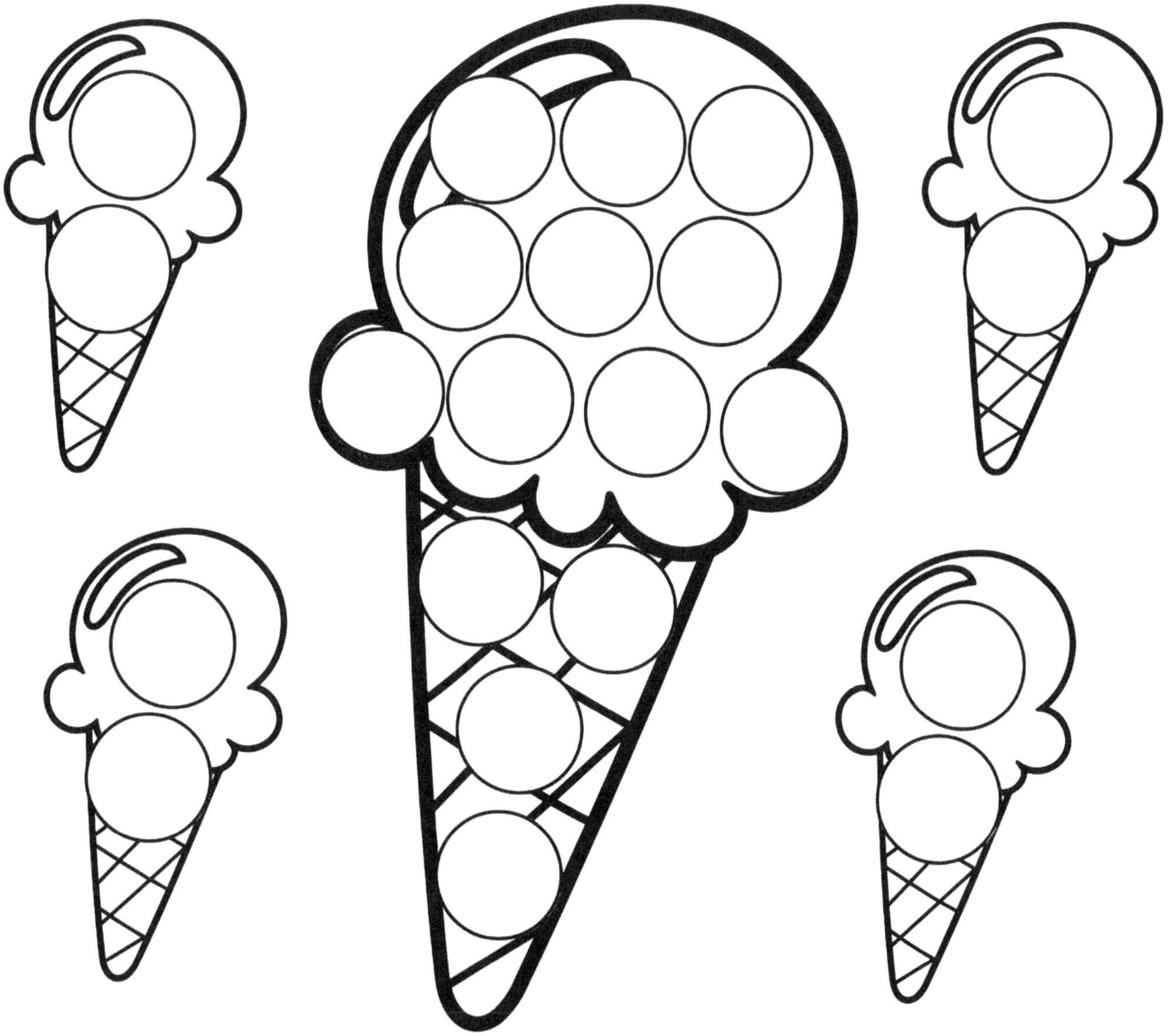

Spell out "Ice Cream" by dotting each letter

I c e

C r e a m

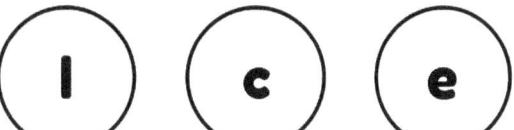

Week 1

Scissor Practice

Cut along the dotted line to practice your scissor skills.

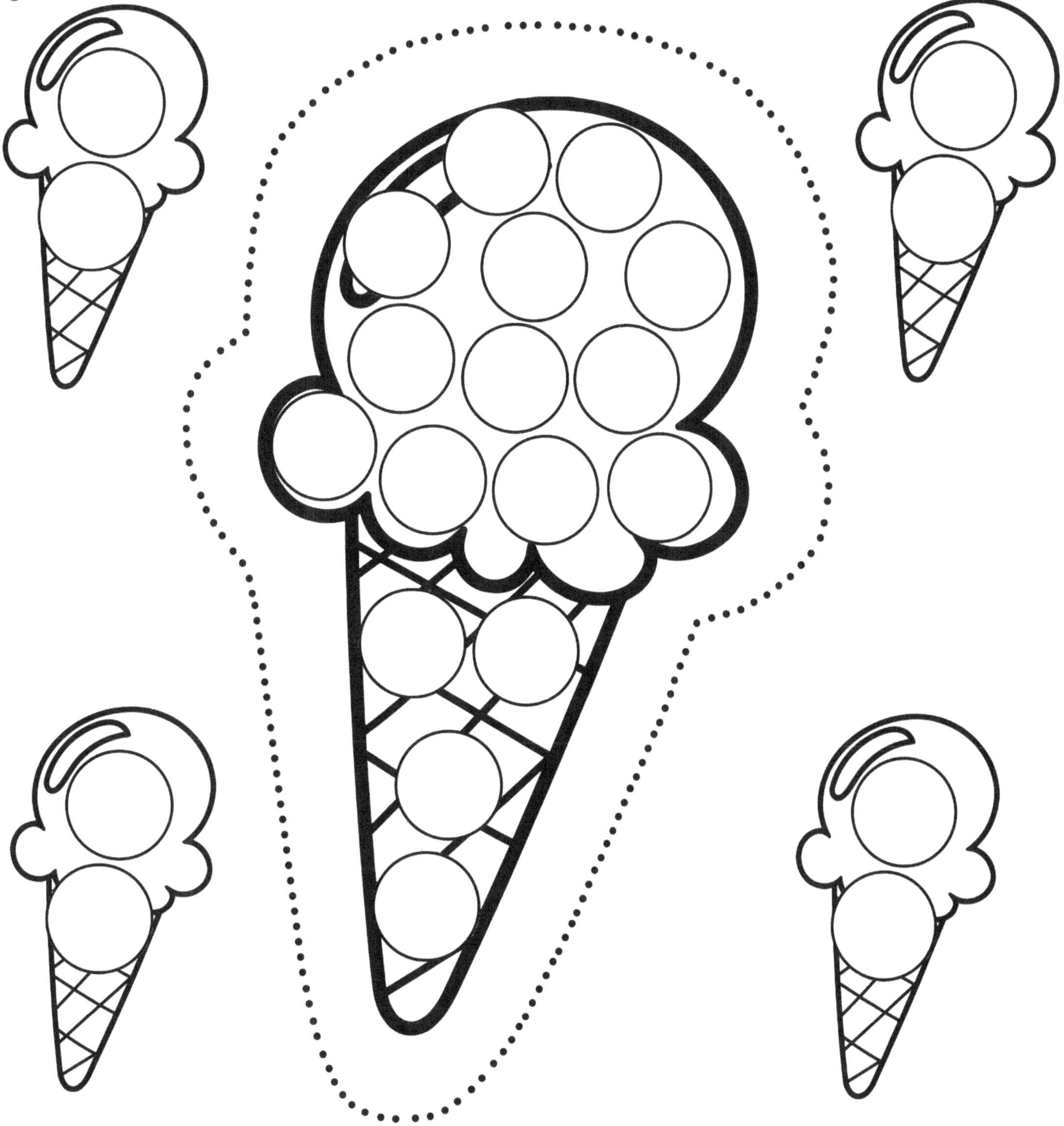

Week 1

Counting

Count the items and write the number below

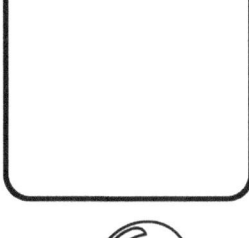

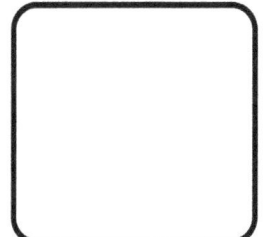

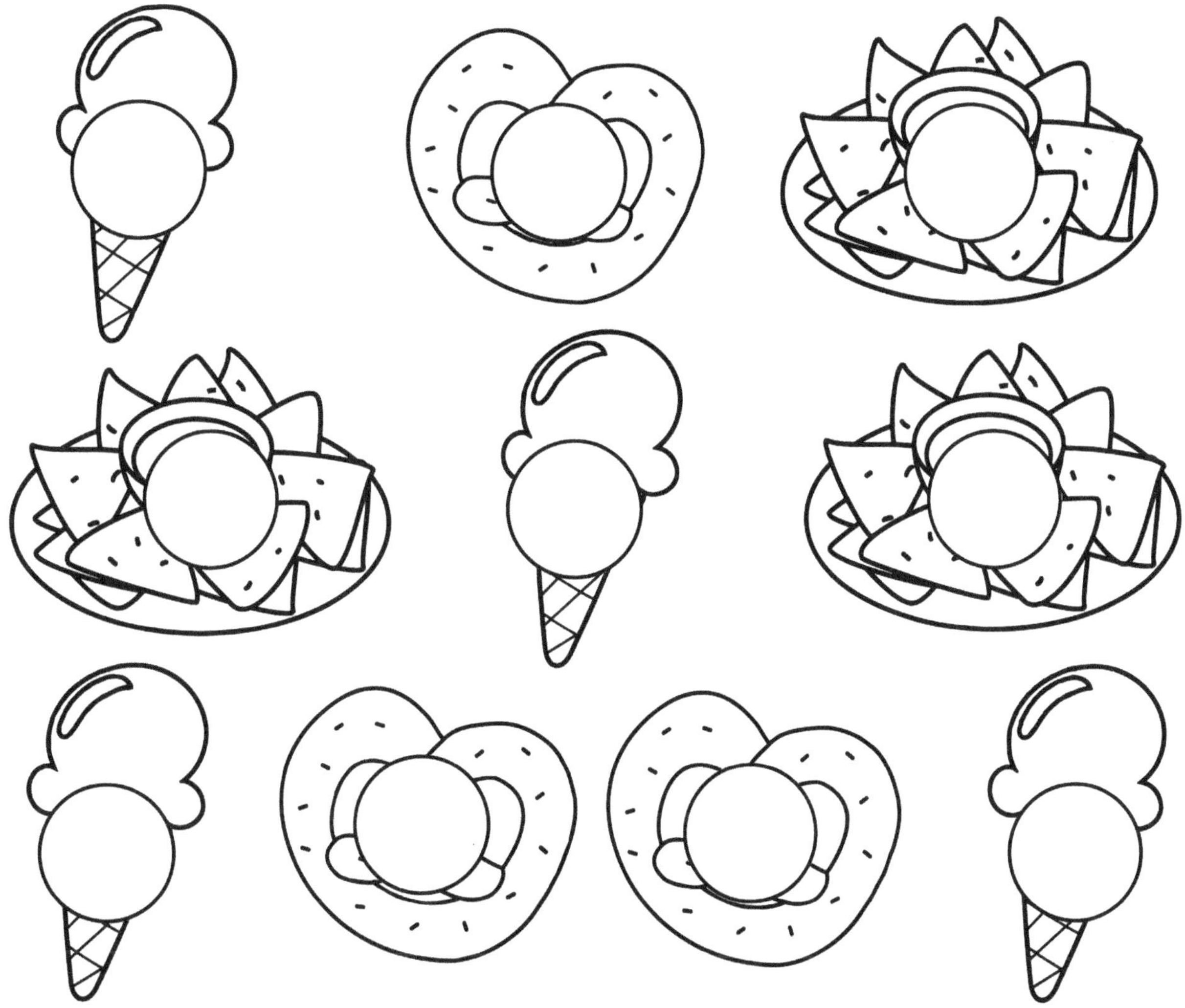

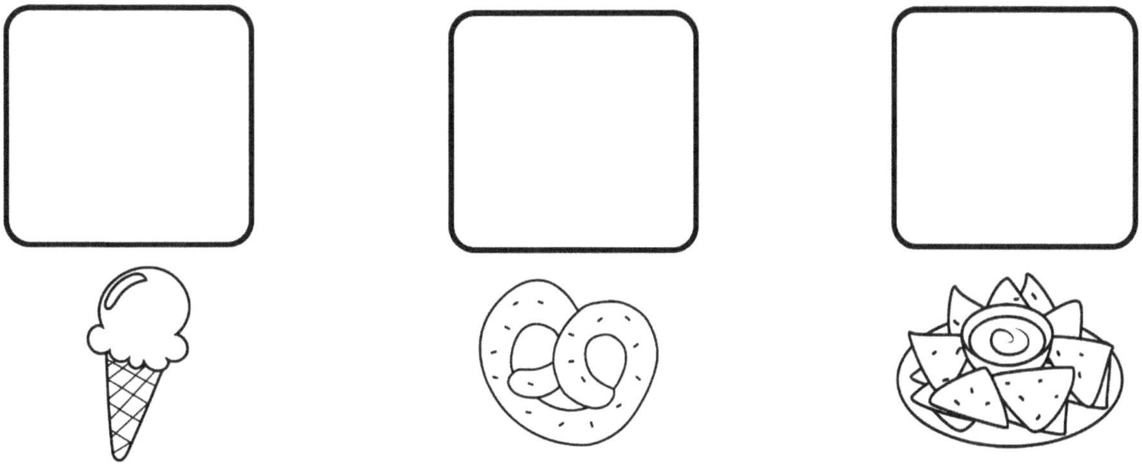

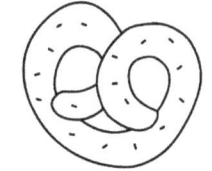

Find the Shadow

Dot the circle to find the shadow

 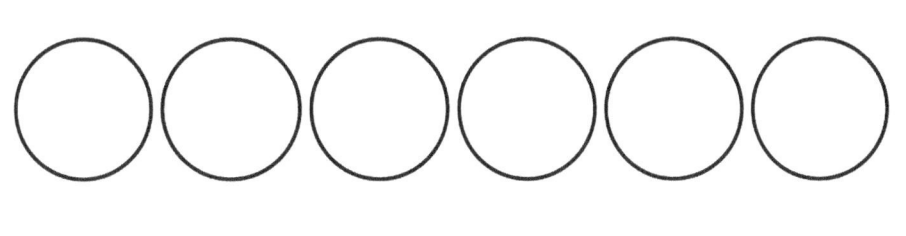 

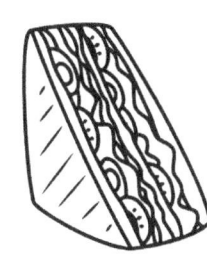 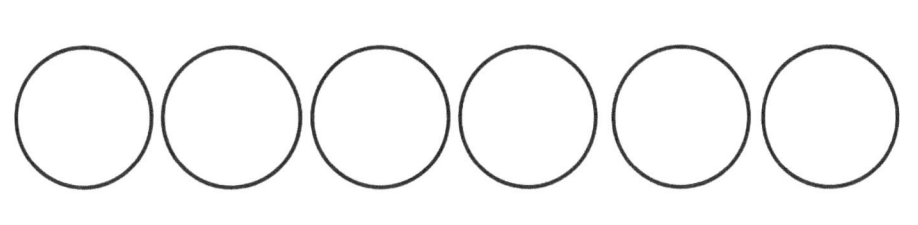 

 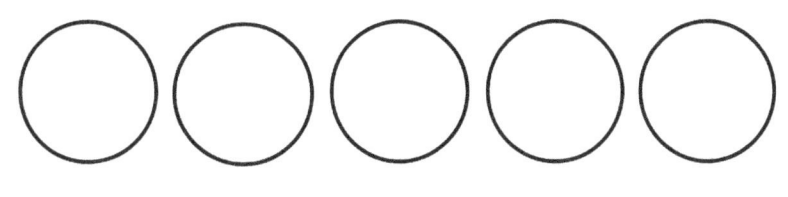 

 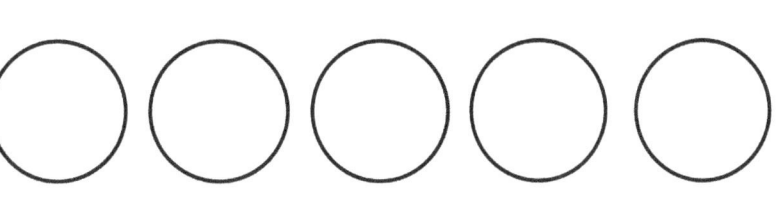 

Milk

MILK

Spell out "Milk" by dotting each letter

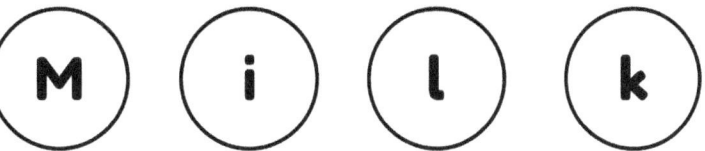

M   i   l   k

Scissor Practice

Cut along the dotted line to practice your scissor skills.

MILK

I Spy

  Find the Milk and dot it.

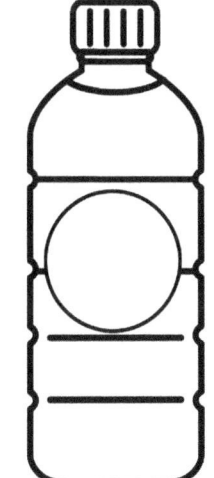 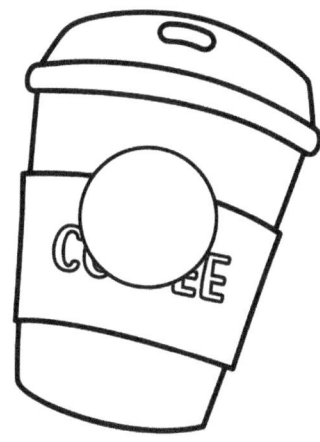 

 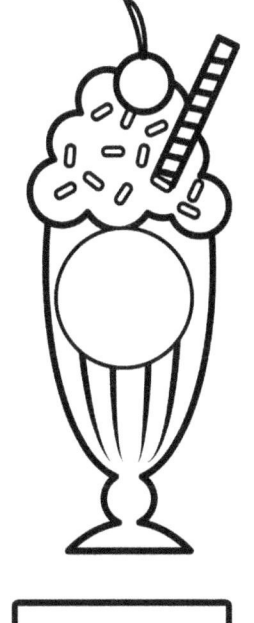 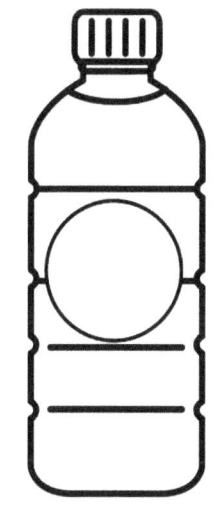

Dot the circles to help the baby find the milk.

Excellent!
The baby found the milk!

MILK

Week 3

Fries

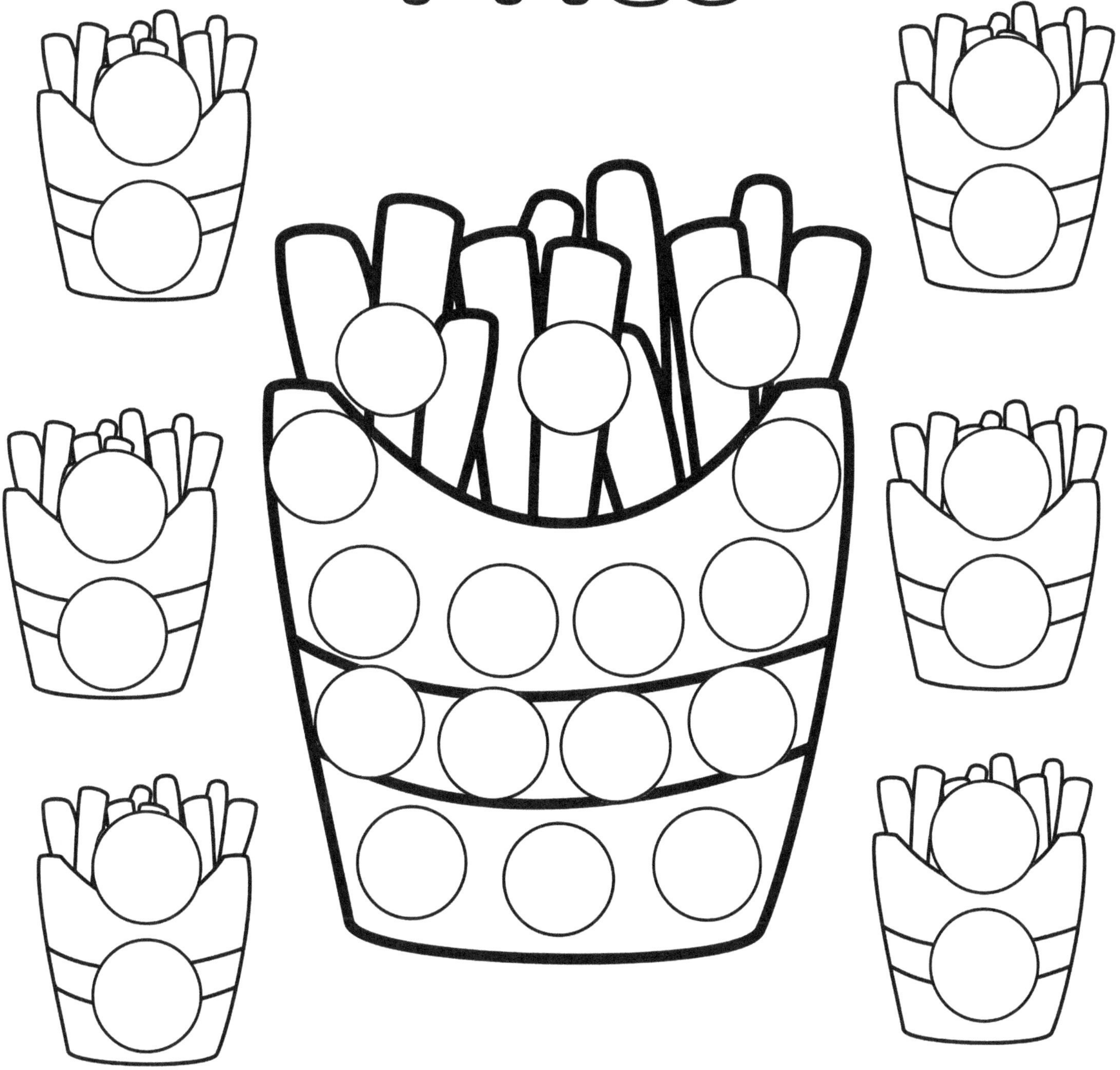

Spell out "Fries" by dotting each letter

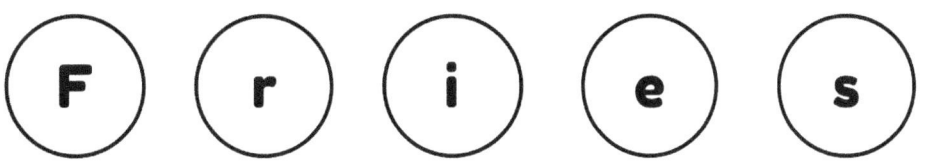

F r i e s

Scissor Practice

Cut along the dotted line to practice your scissor skills.

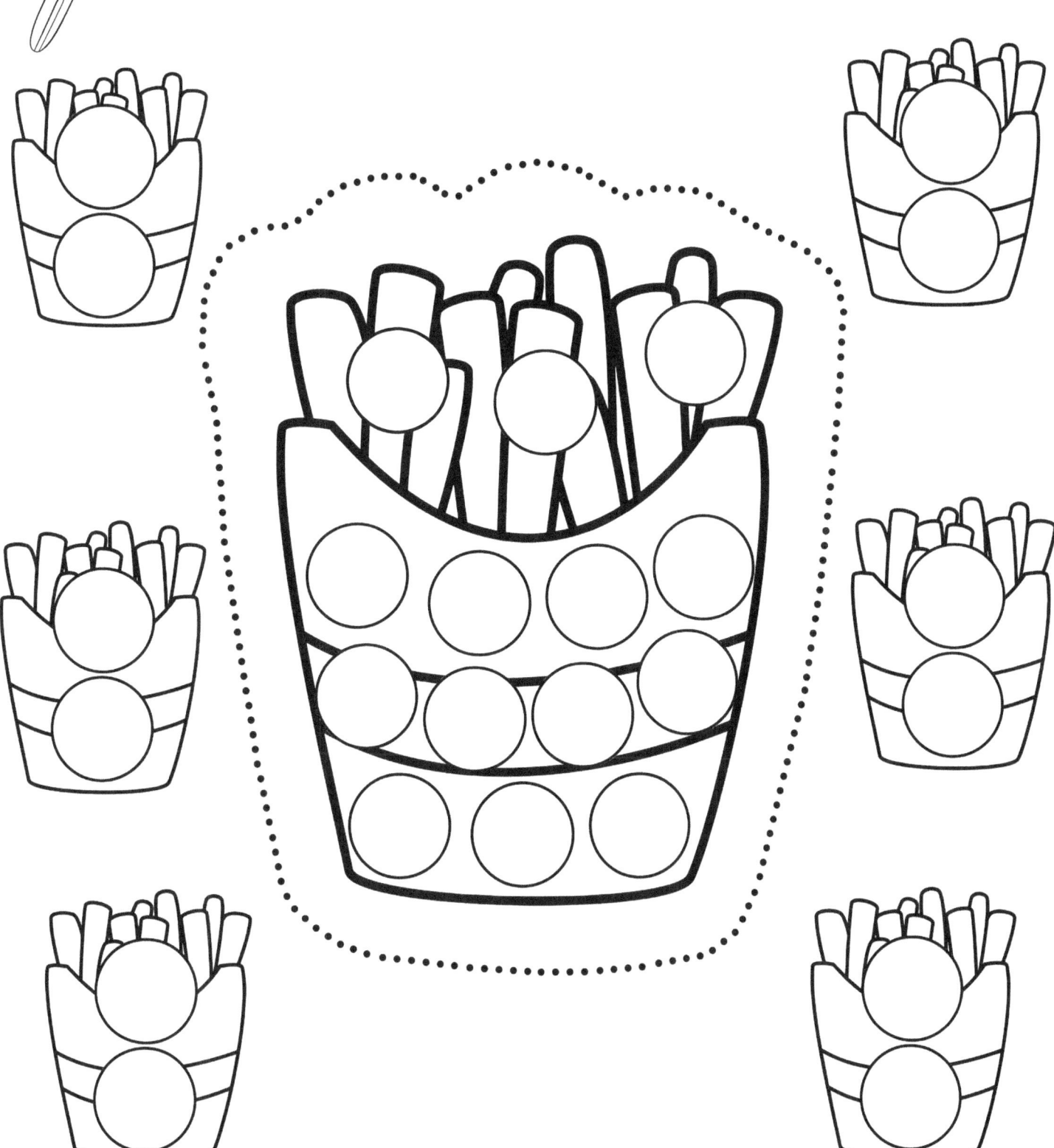

Week 3

Counting

Count the items and write the number below

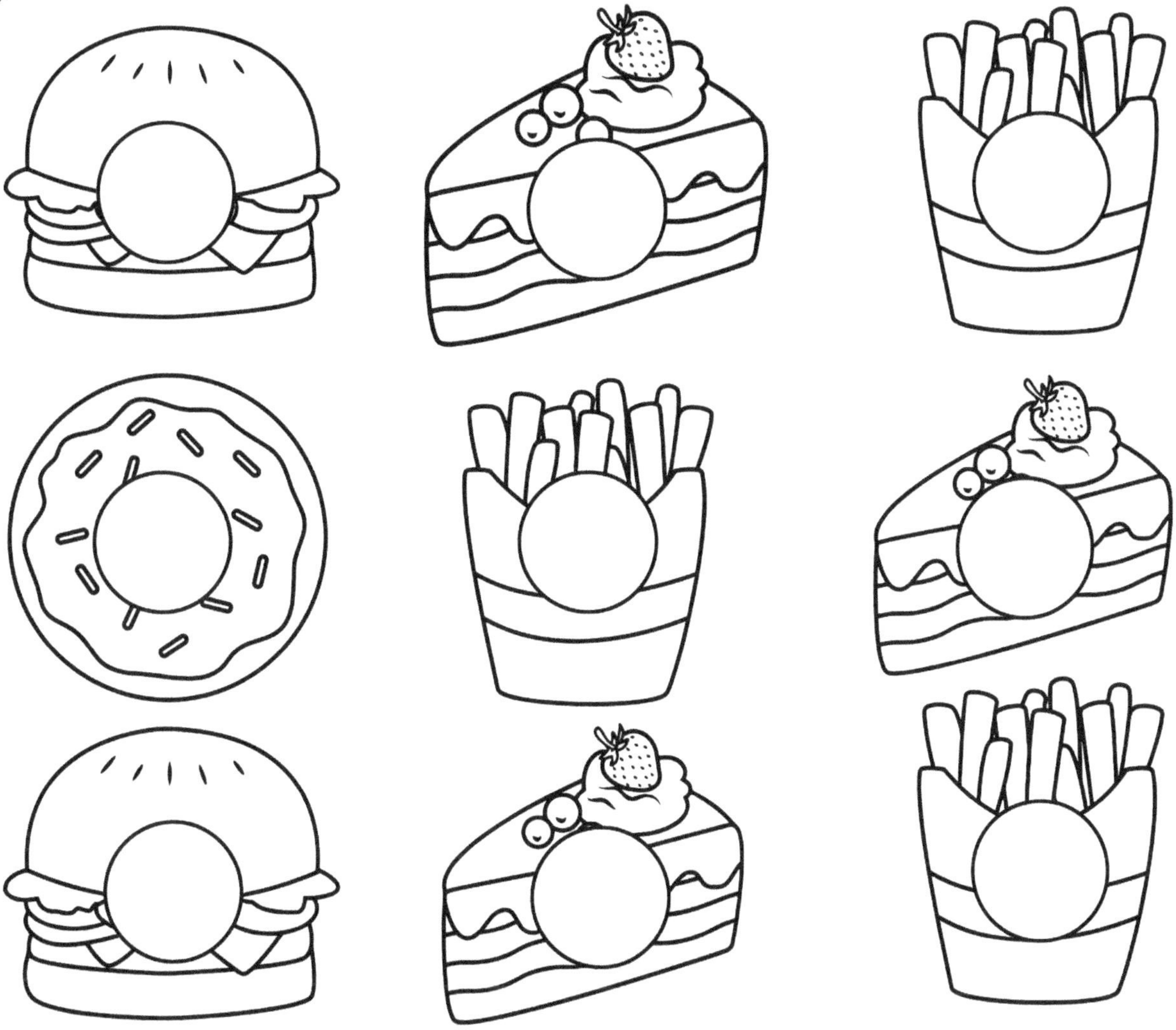

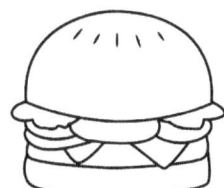

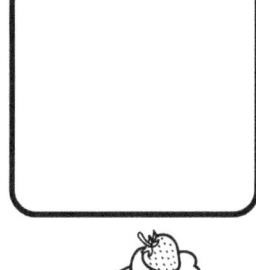

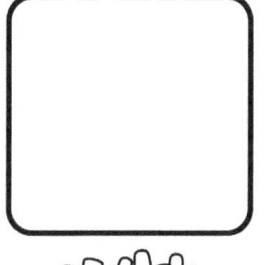

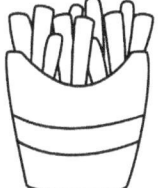

Find the Shadow

Dot the circle to find the shadow

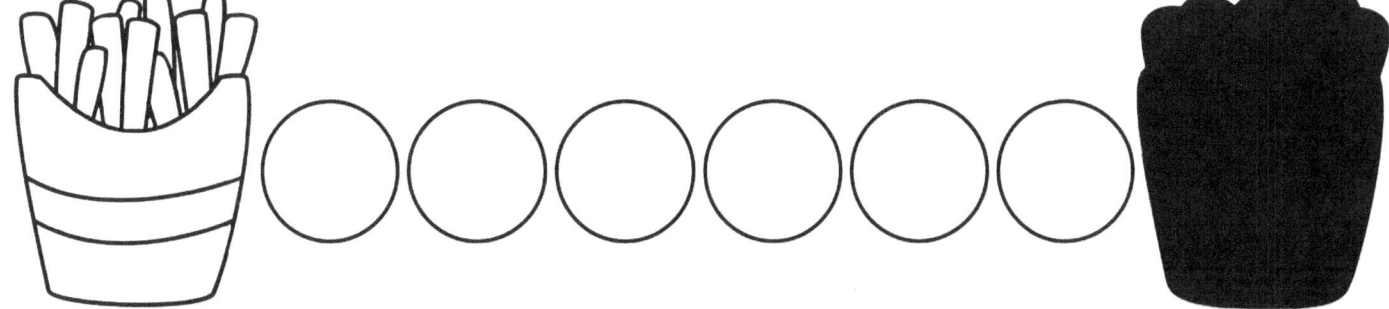

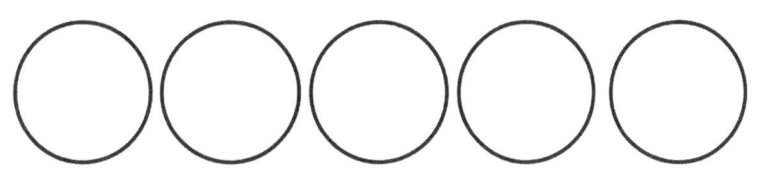

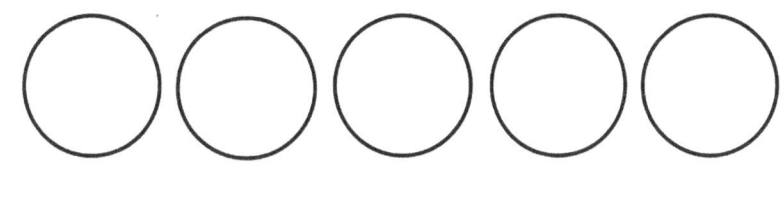

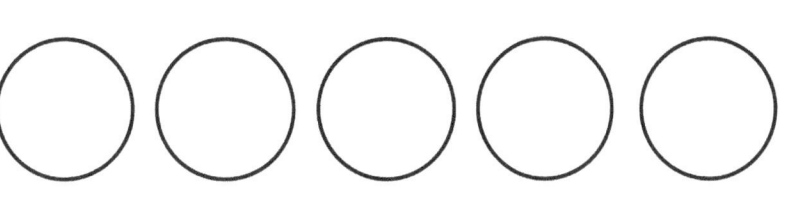

Water

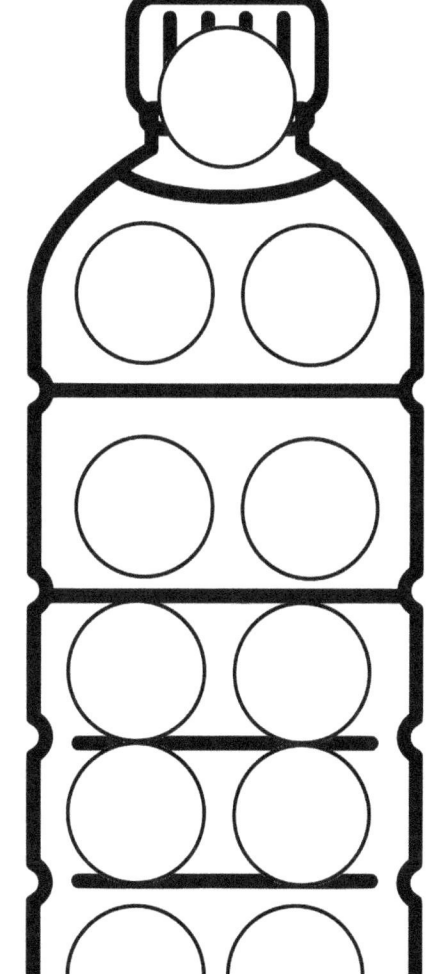

Spell out "Water" by dotting each letter

W   a   t   e   r

Week 4

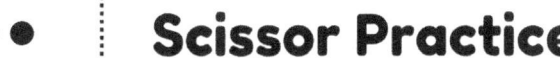

Scissor Practice

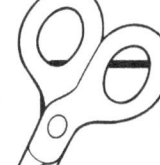

Cut along the dotted line to practice your scissor skills.

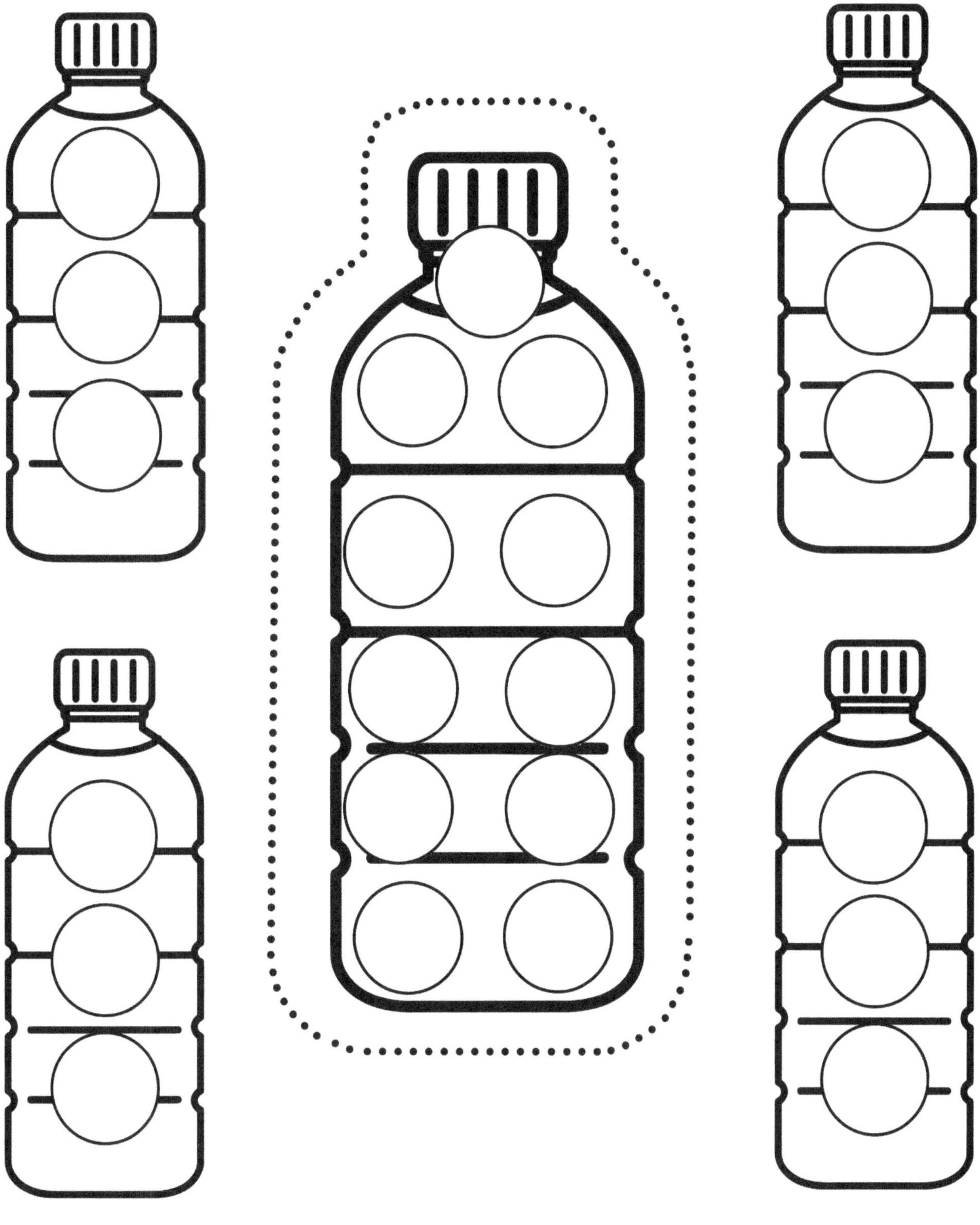

I Spy

I SPY Find the Water and dot it.

Maze

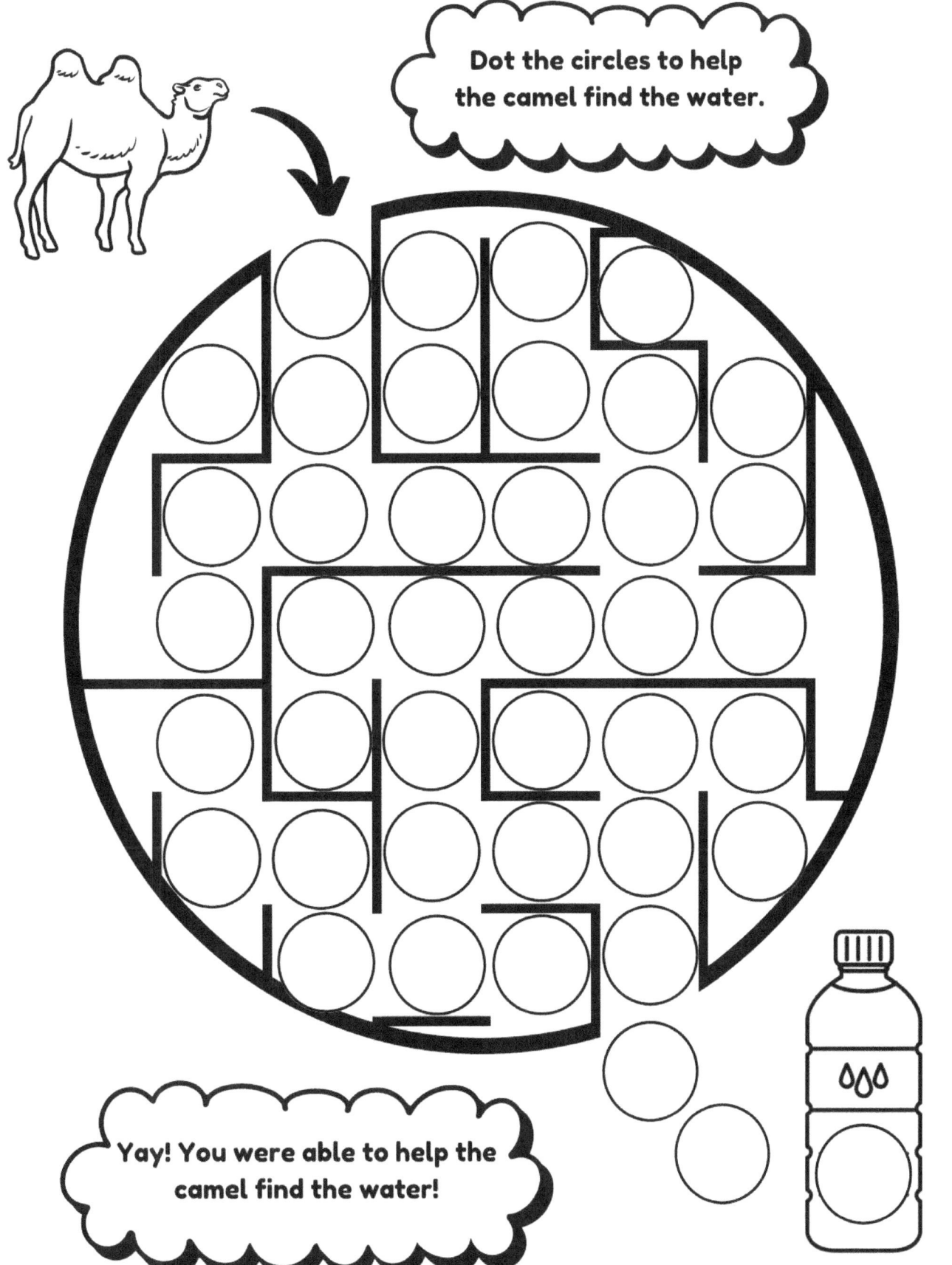

Dot the circles to help the camel find the water.

Yay! You were able to help the camel find the water!

Chocolate

Spell out "Chocolate" by dotting each letter

C h o c o l a t e

Week 5

Scissor Practice

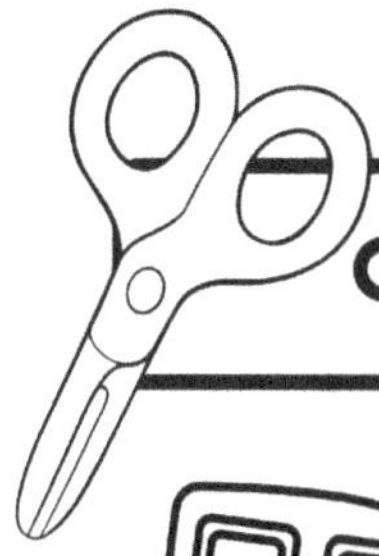

Cut along the dotted line to practice your scissor skills.

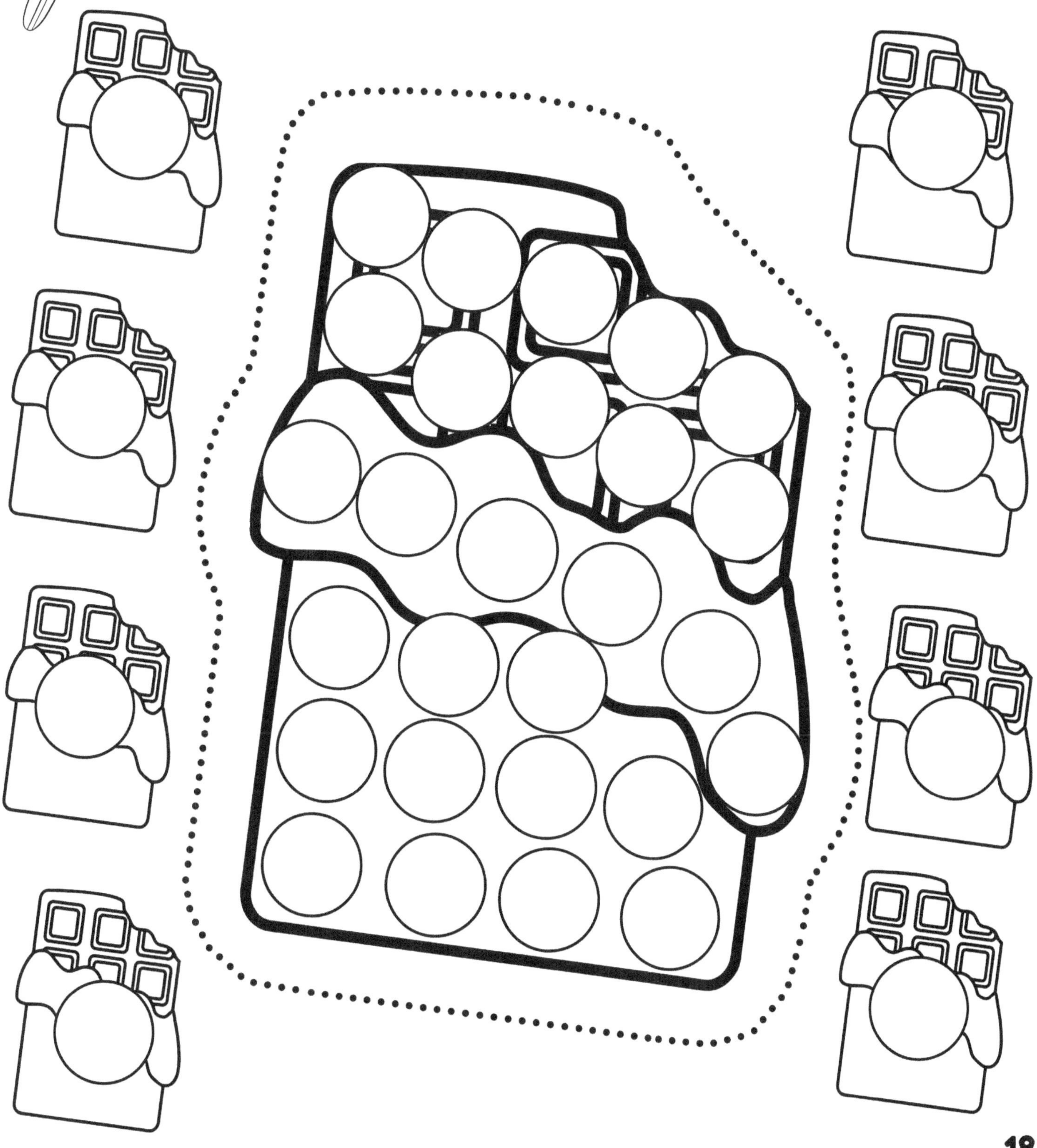

Counting

Count the items and write the number below

19

Week 5

Find the Shadow

Dot the circle to find the shadow

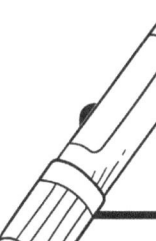

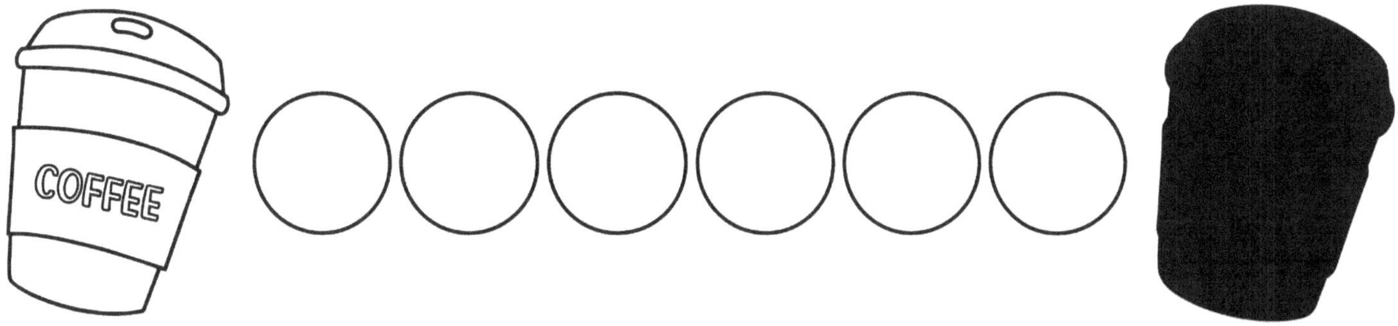

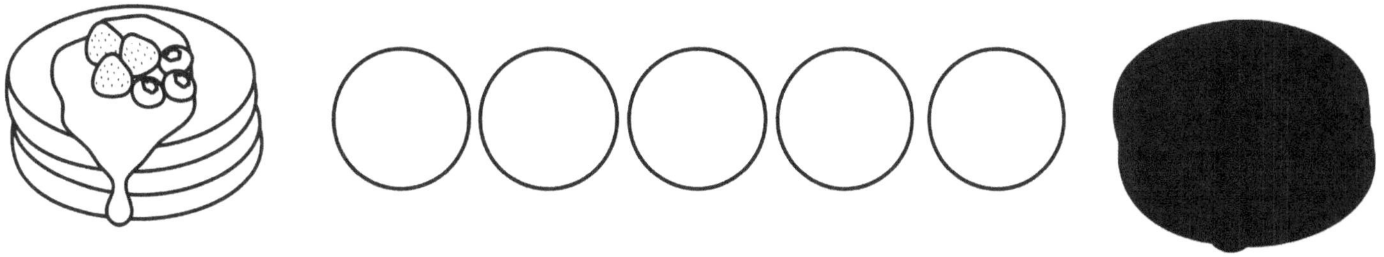

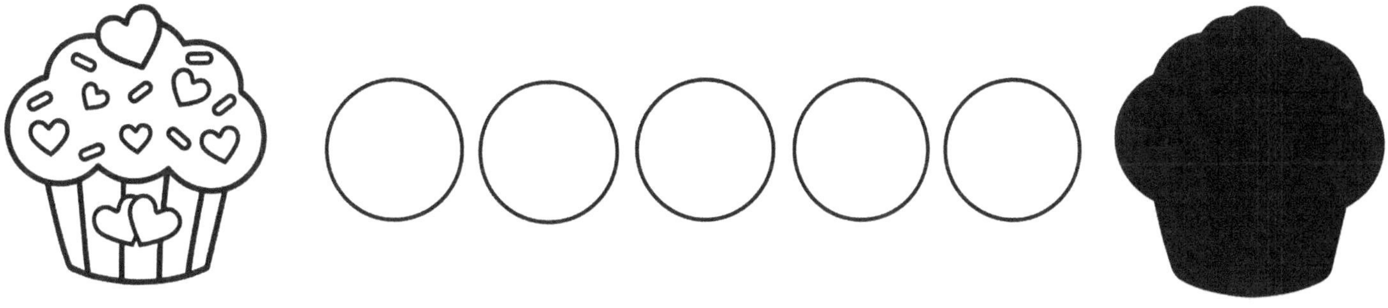

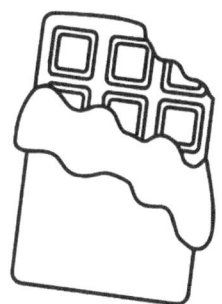

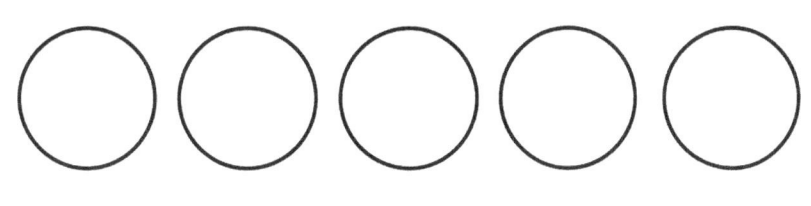

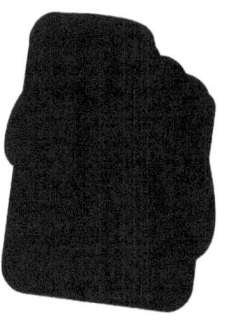

Coffee

Spell out "Coffee" by dotting each letter

C o f f e e

Week 6

Scissor Practice

Cut along the dotted line to practice your scissor skills.

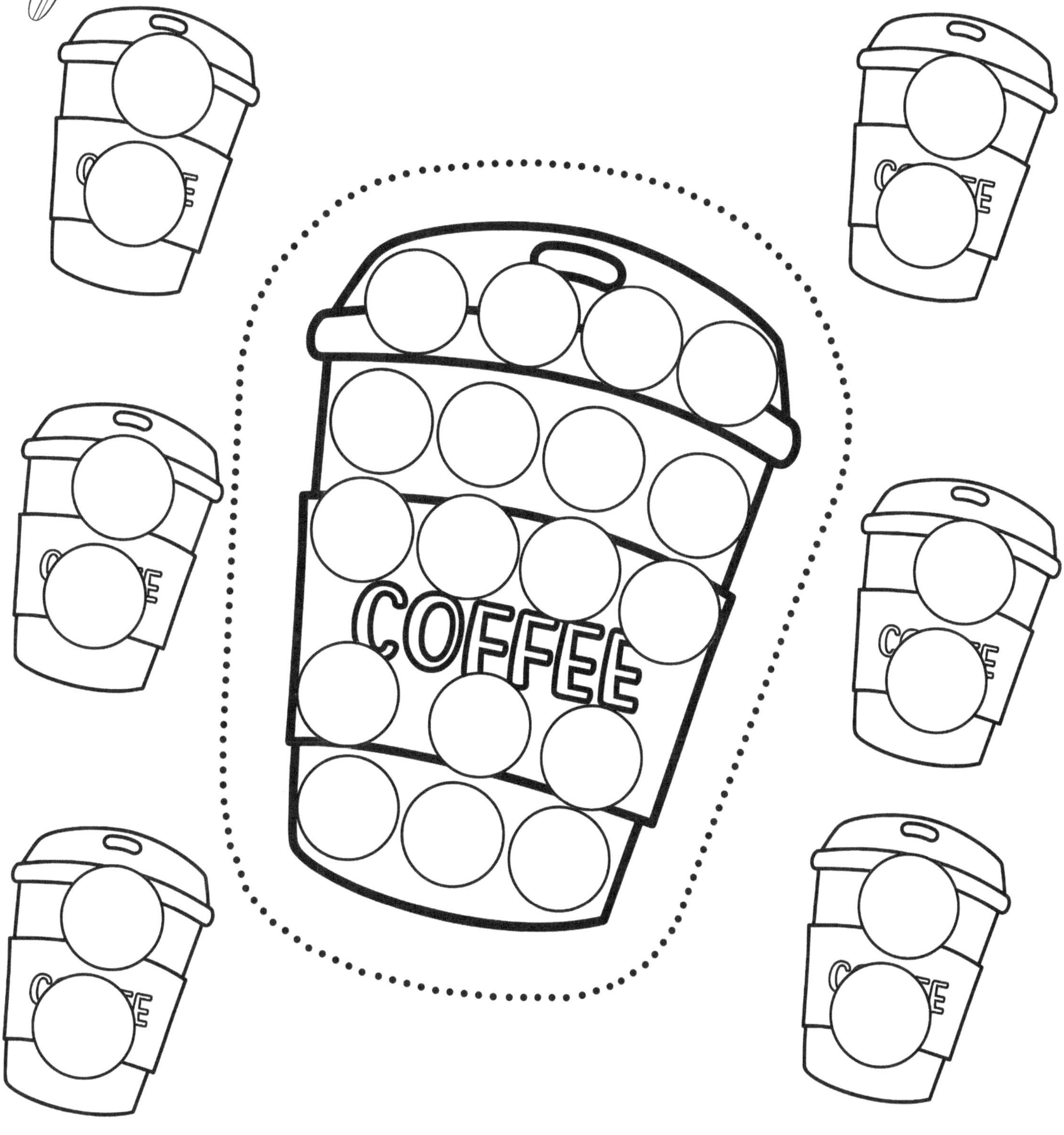

COFFEE

I Spy

Find the Coffee and dot it.

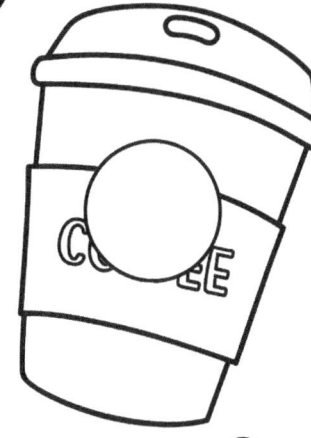

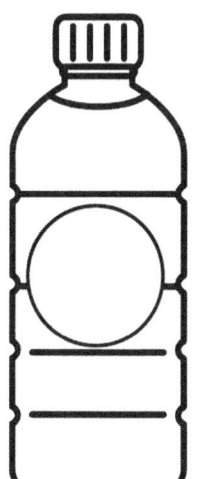

I Spy

Dot the circles to help the teacher find a coffee.

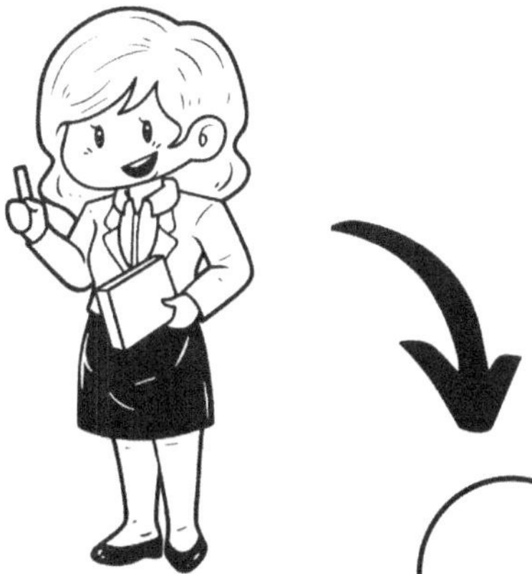

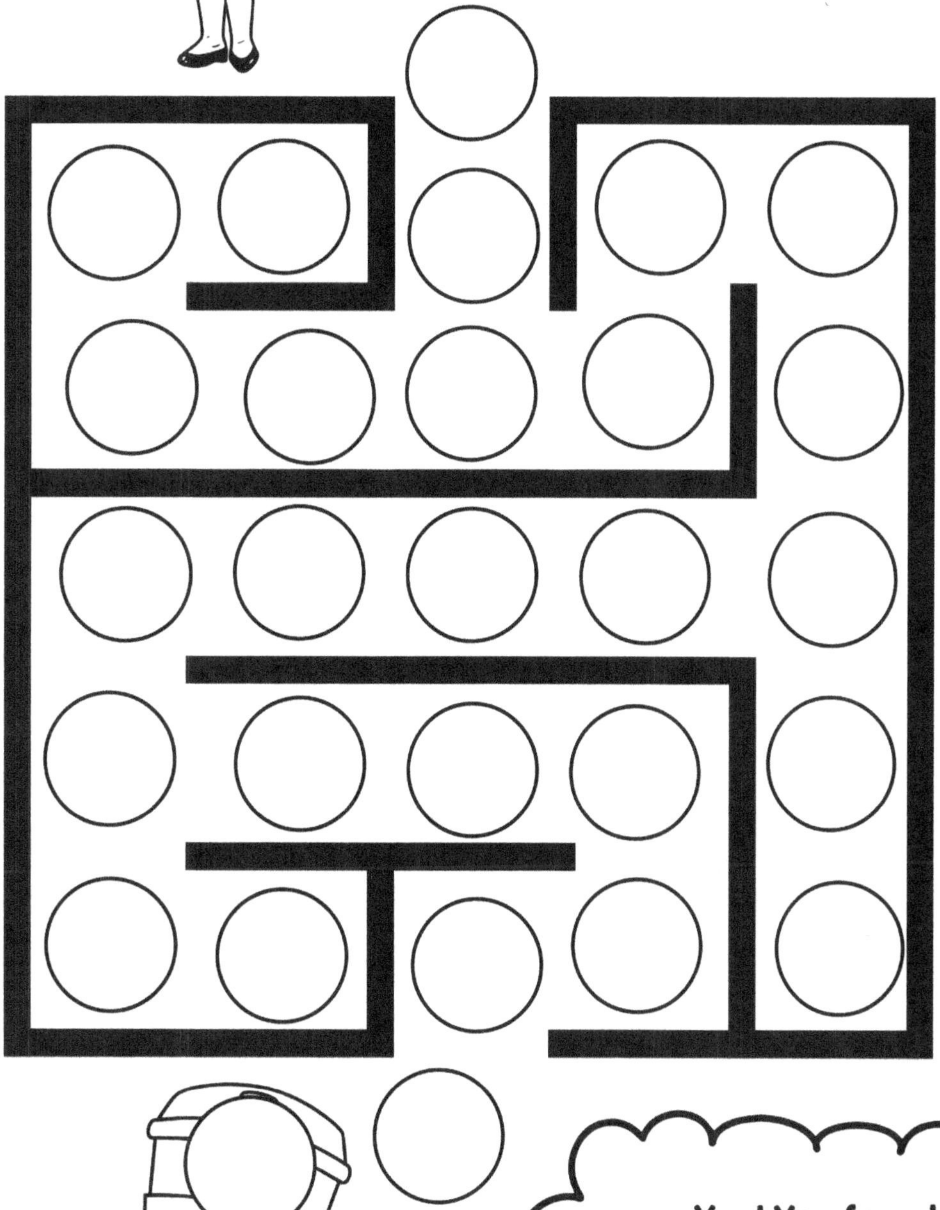

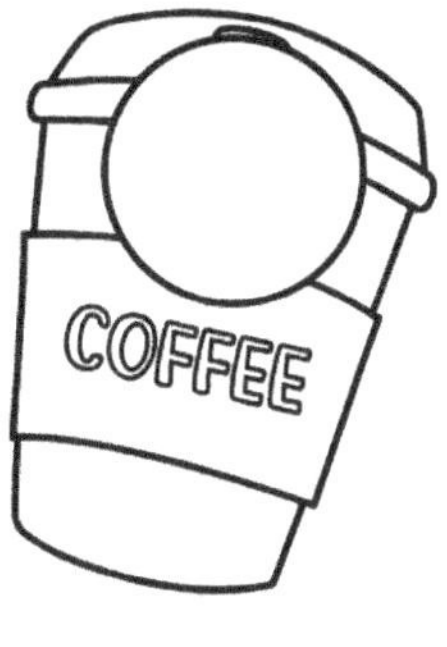

Yay! You found the coffee.

COFFEE

Week 7

Burger

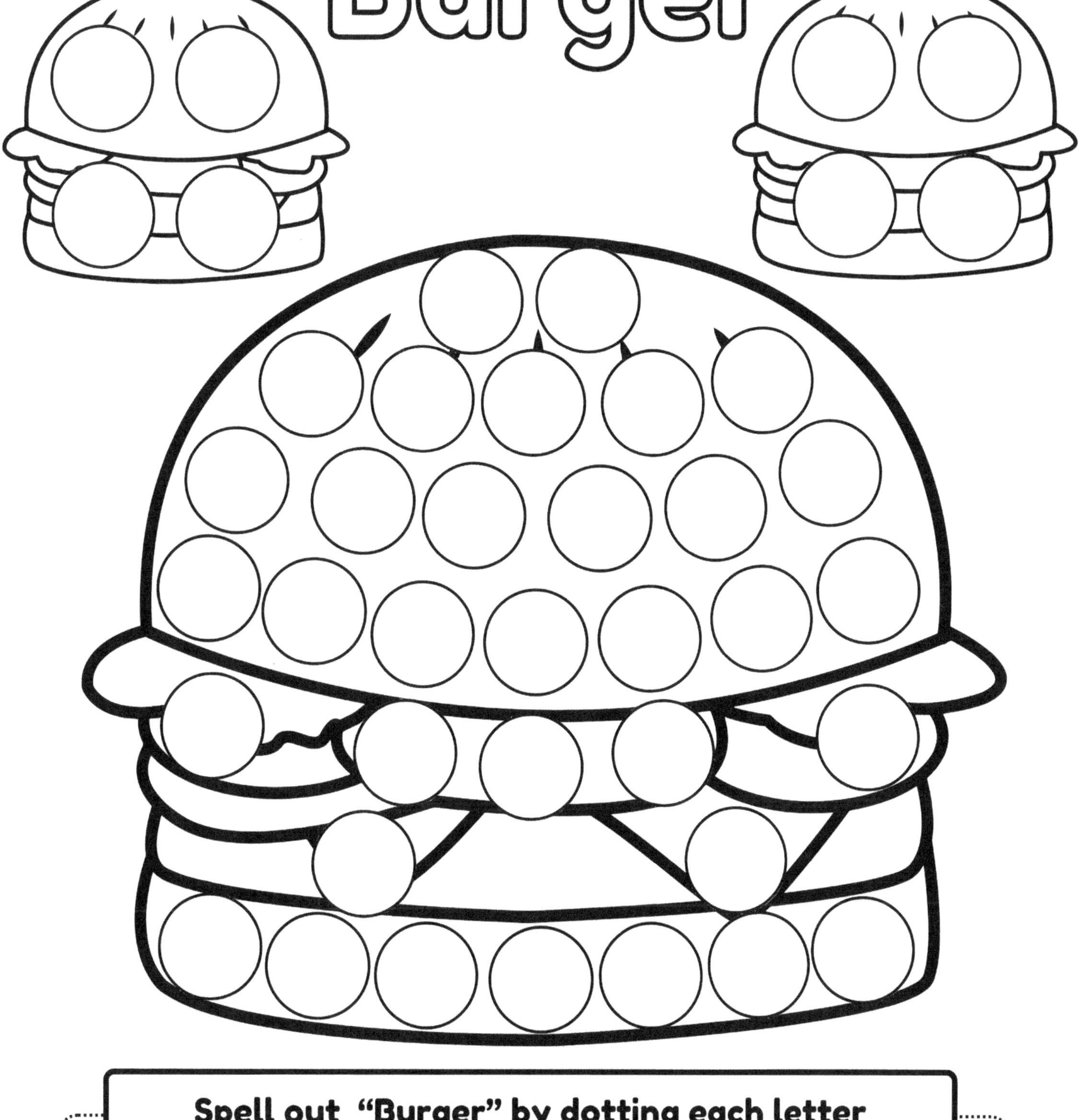

Spell out "Burger" by dotting each letter

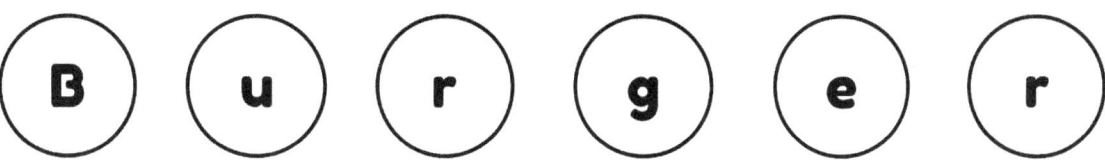

B u r g e r

Scissor Practice

Cut along the dotted line to practice your scissor skills.

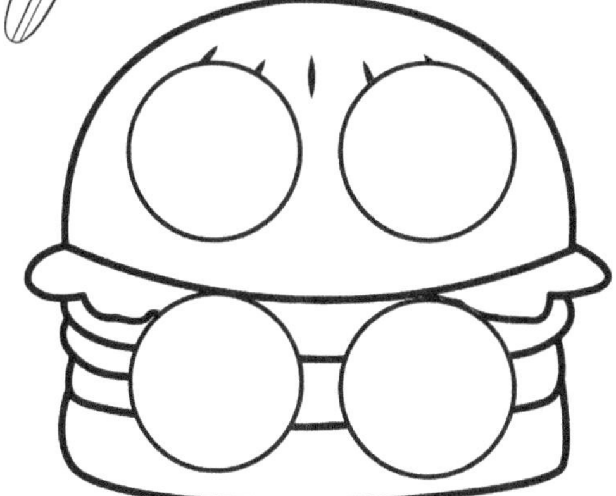

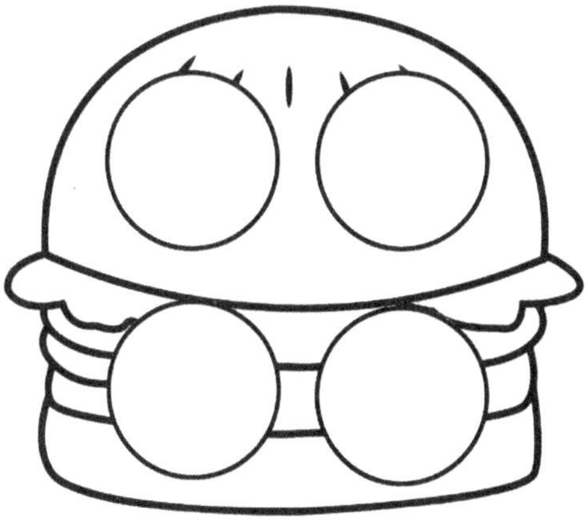

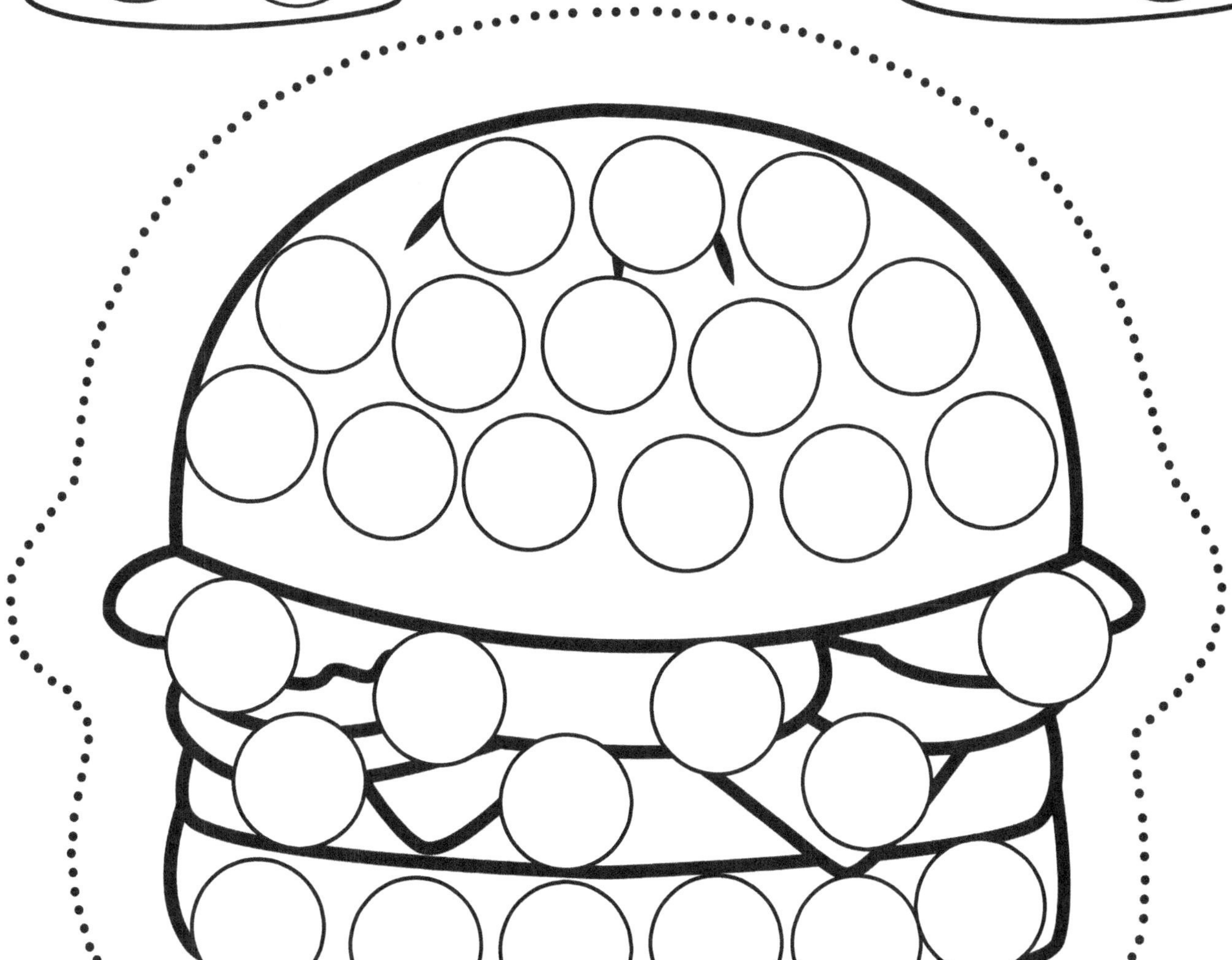

Counting

Count the items and write the number below

Dot the circle to find the shadow

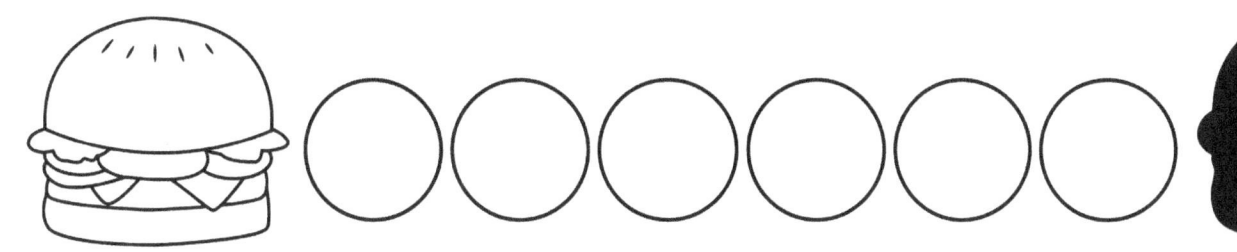 

 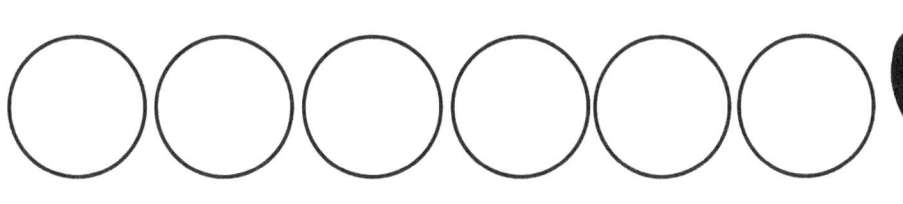 

 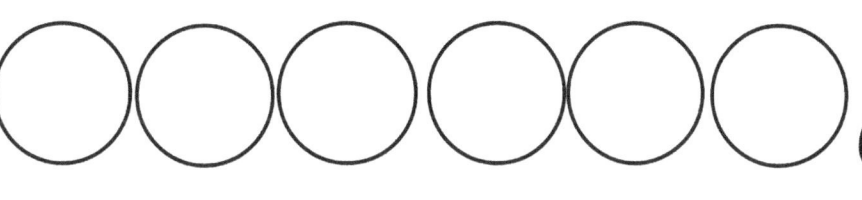 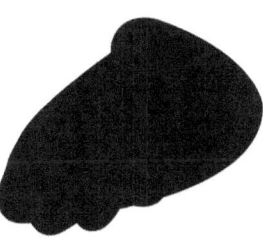

 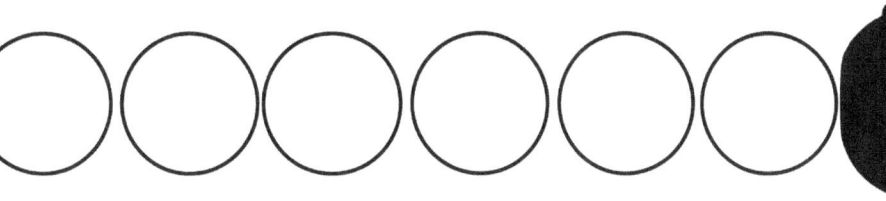

Bubble Tea

Spell out "Bubble Tea" by dotting each letter

B u b b l e

T e a

Week 8

Scissor Practice

Cut along the dotted line to practice your scissor skills.

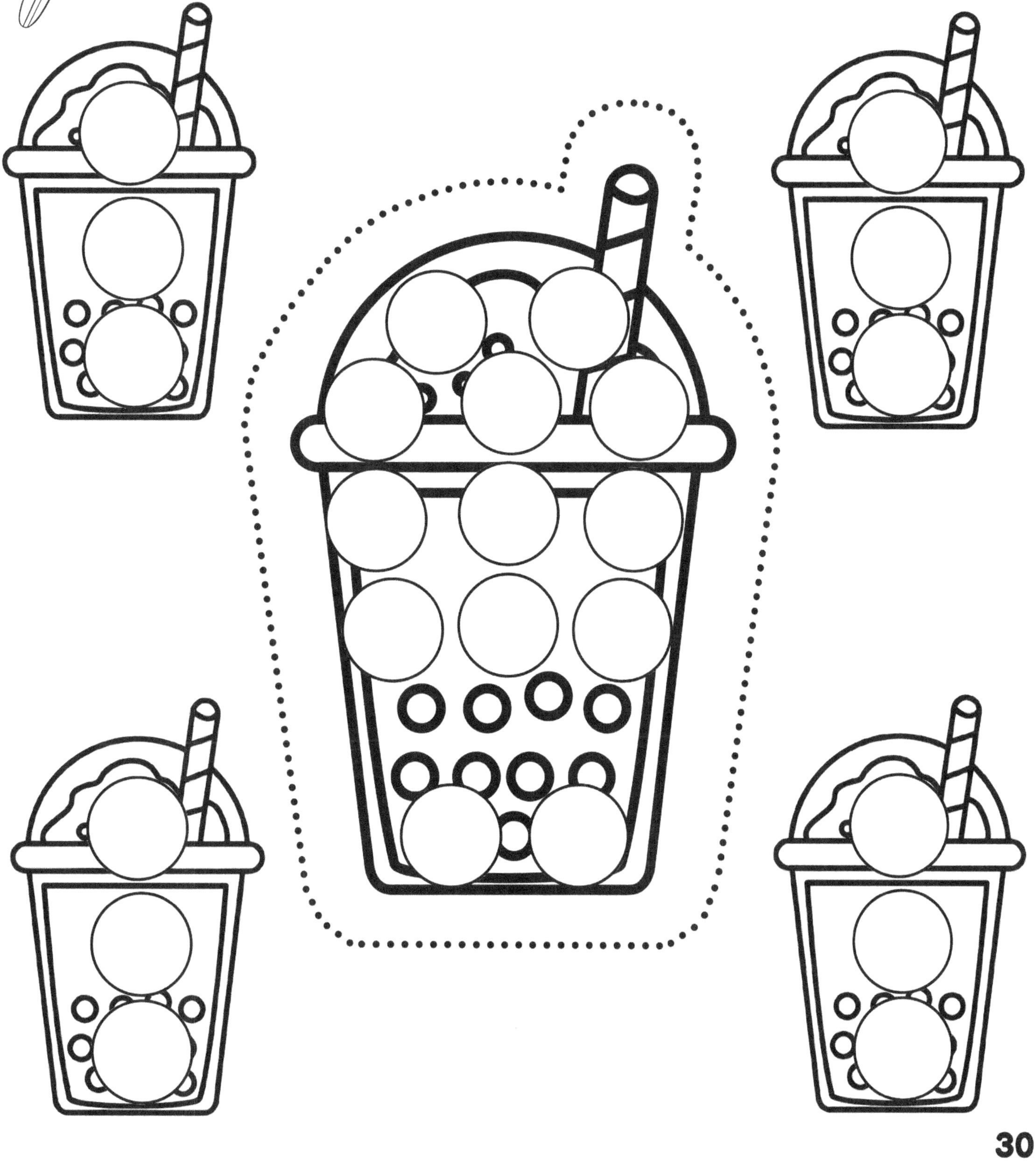

I Spy

 **Find the Bubble Tea and dot it.**

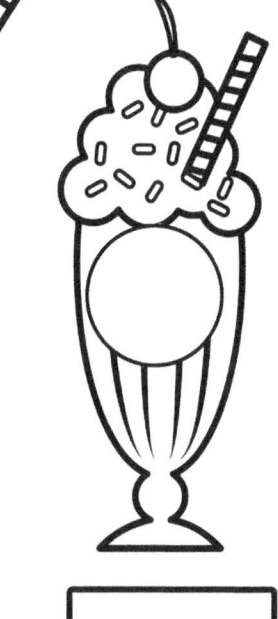

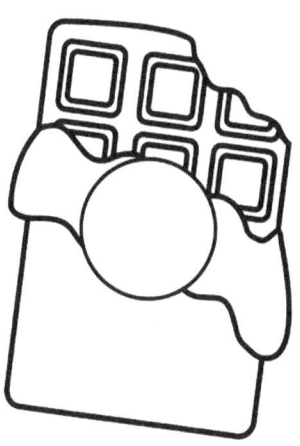

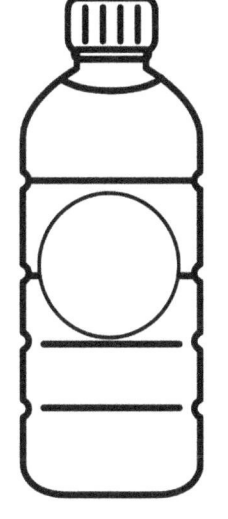

MILK

COFFEE

Maze

Dot the circles to help Kayla find a bubble tea.

Impressive!
Kayla was able to find the Bubble Tea!

Sausage

Spell out "Sausage" by dotting each letter

S a u s a g e

Week 9

Scissor Practice

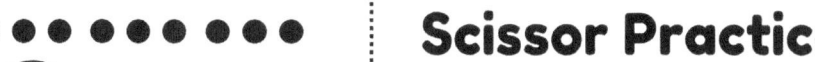

Cut along the dotted line to practice your scissor skills.

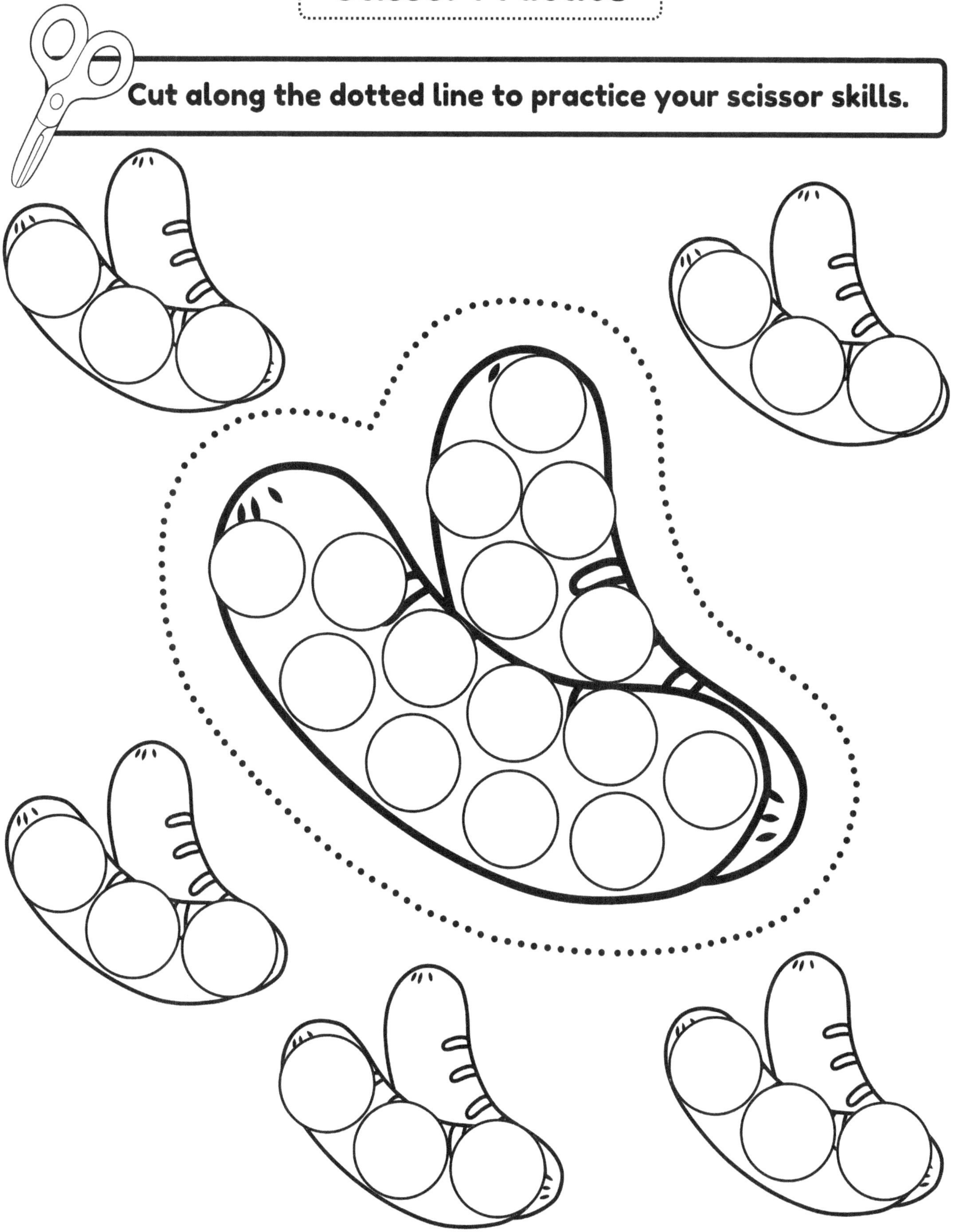

Counting

Count the items and write the number below

Dot the circle to find the shadow

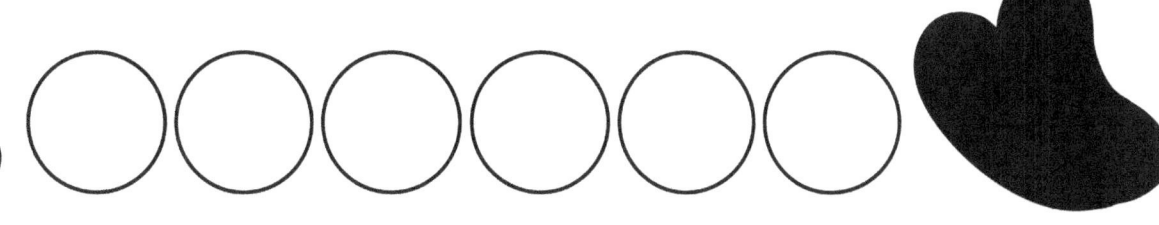

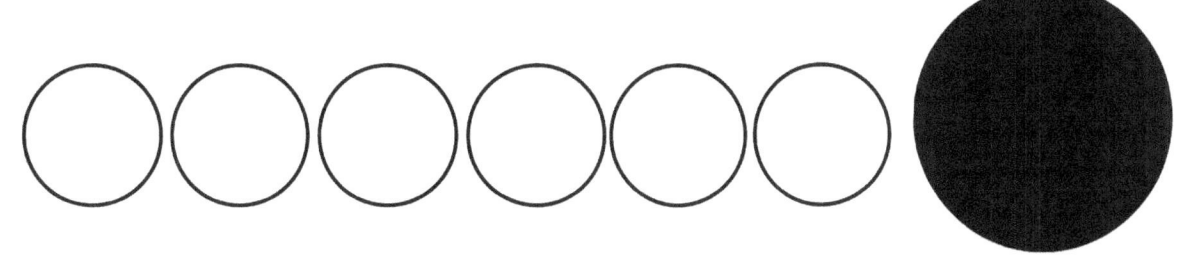

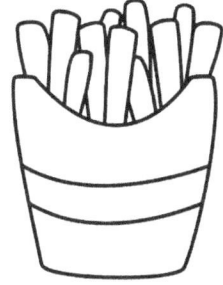
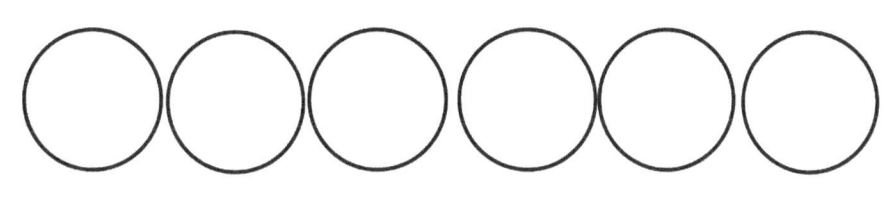

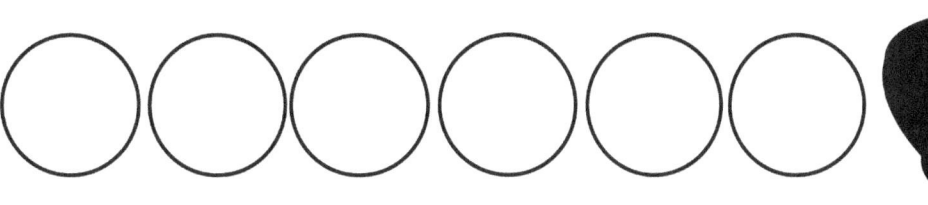

Soda

Spell out "Soda" by dotting each letter

S   o   d   a

Scissor Practice

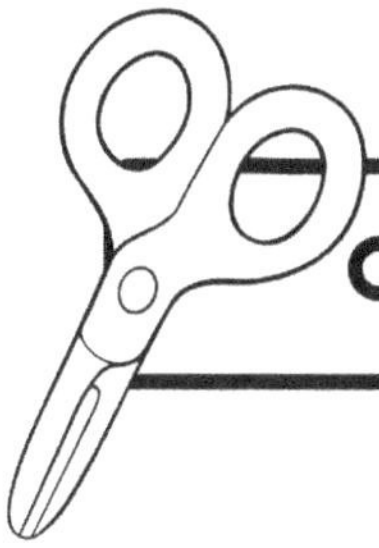

Cut along the dotted line to practice your scissor skills.

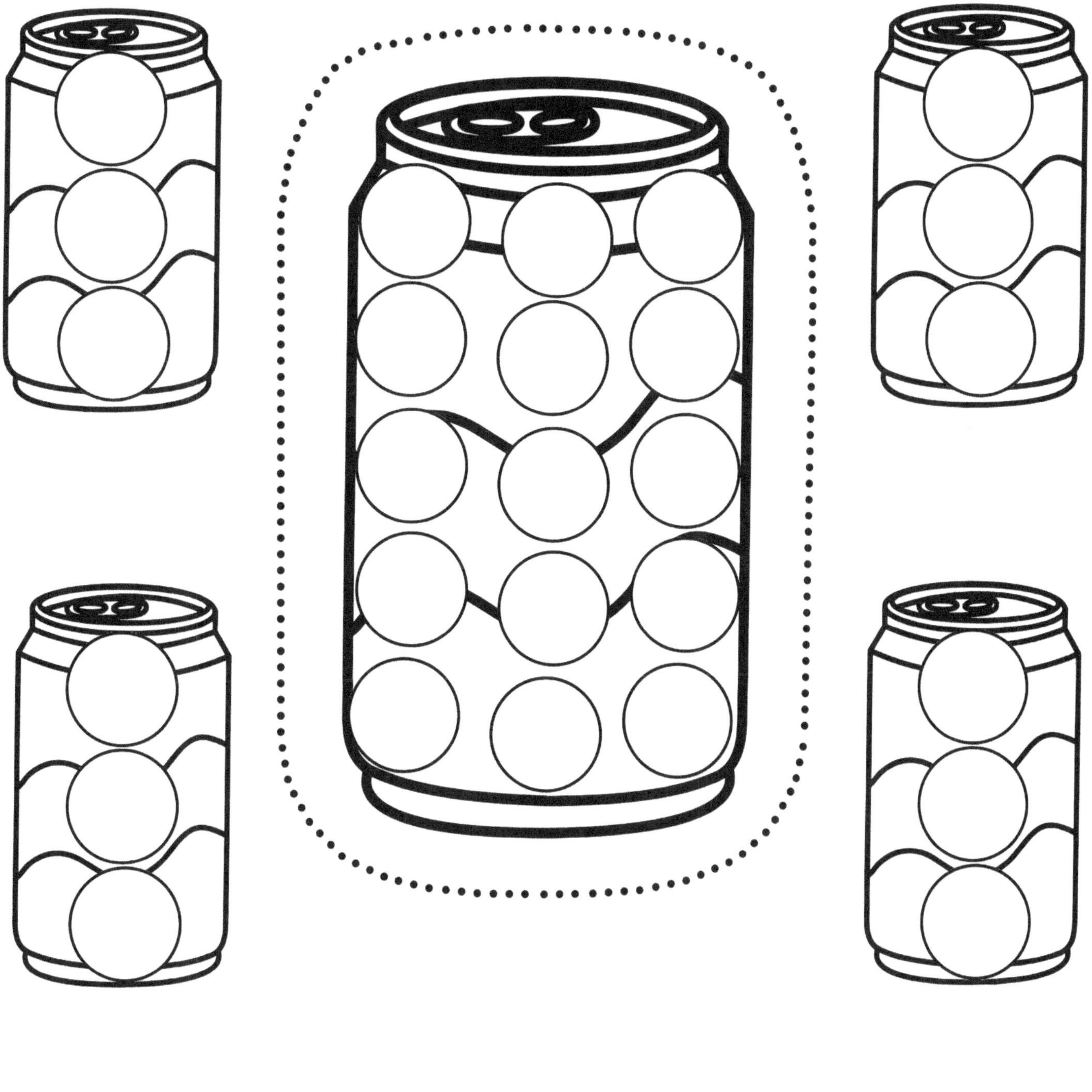

I Spy

I SPY Find the Soda and dot it.

Maze

Dot the circles to help John find the soda.

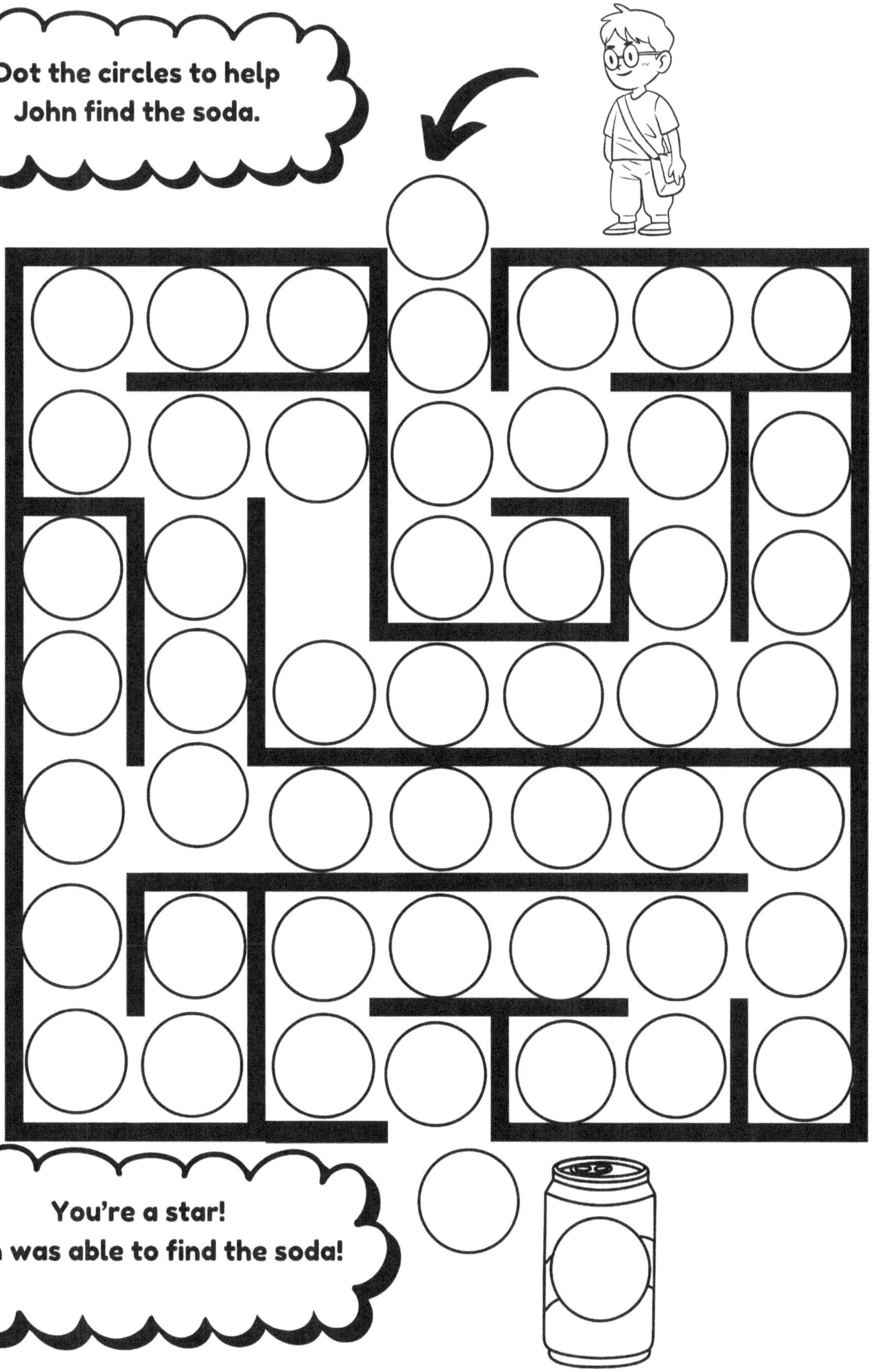

You're a star!
John was able to find the soda!

Pretzel

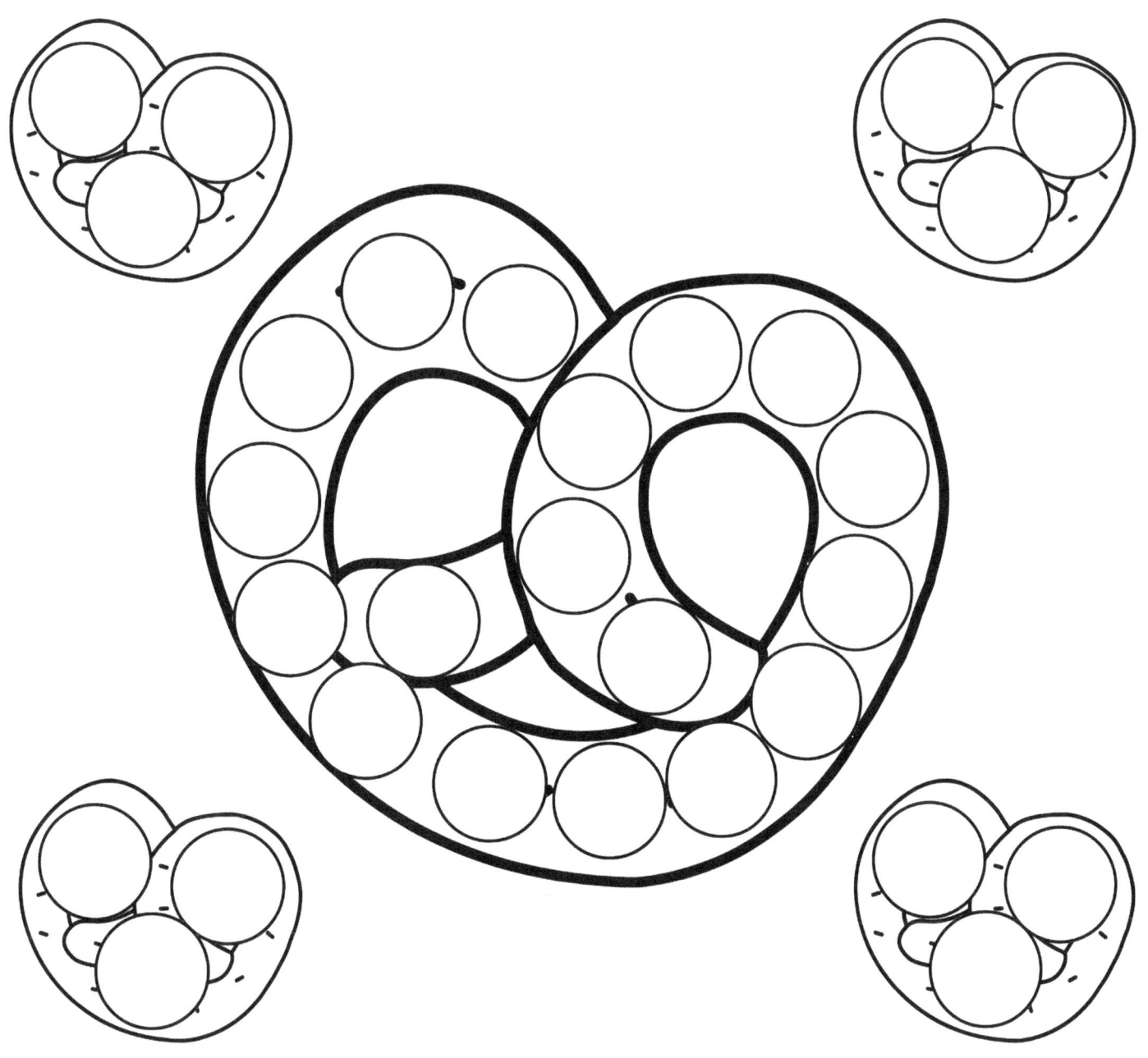

Spell out "Pretzel" by dotting each letter

(P) (r) (e) (t) (z) (e) (l)

Scissor Practice

Cut along the dotted line to practice your scissor skills.

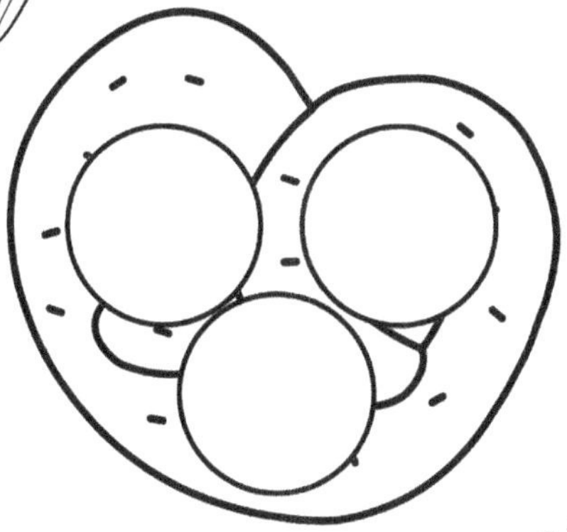

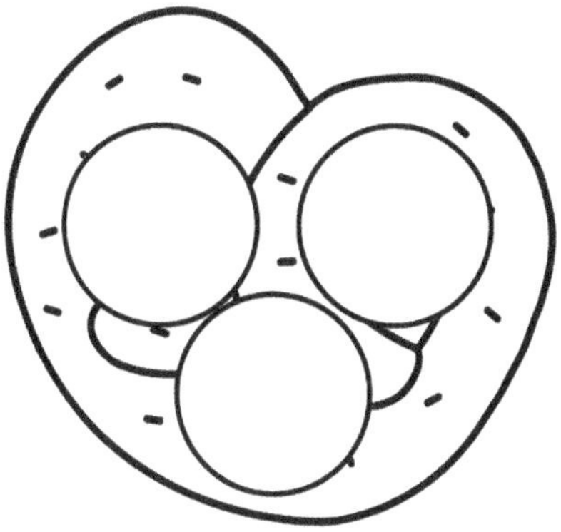

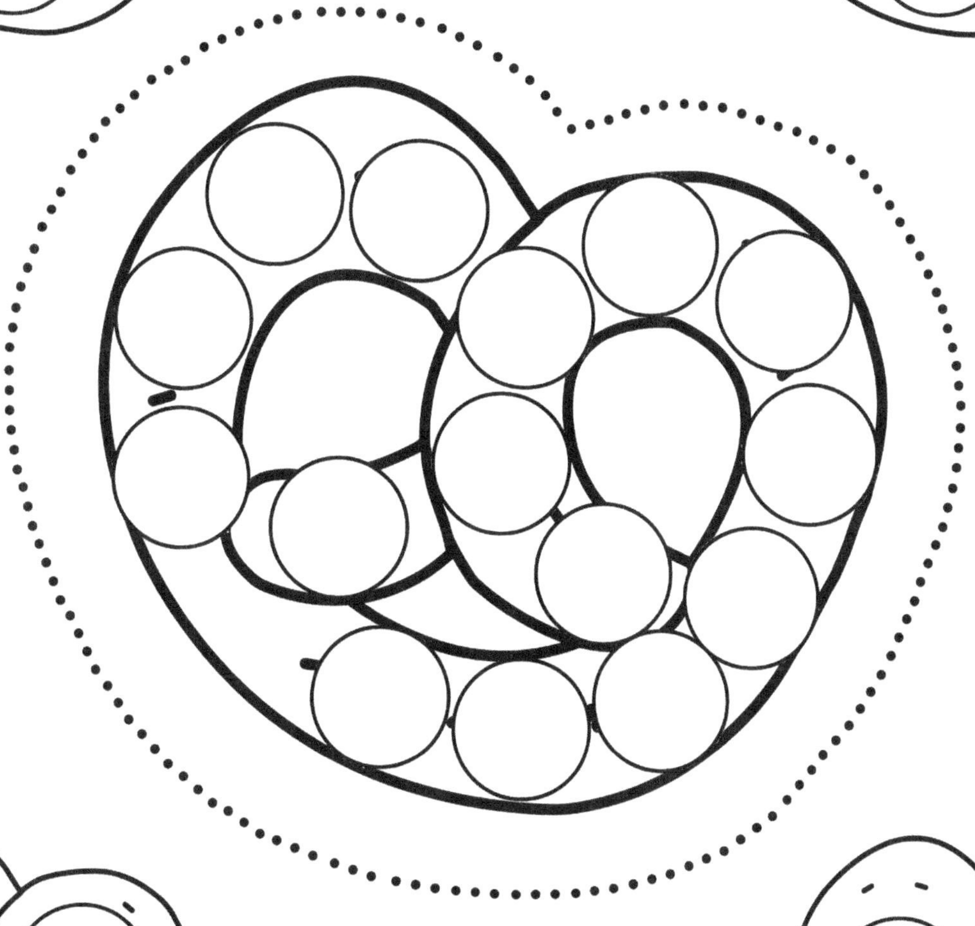

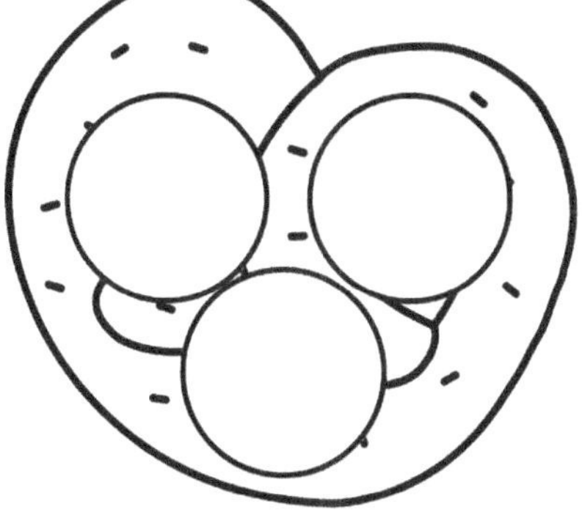

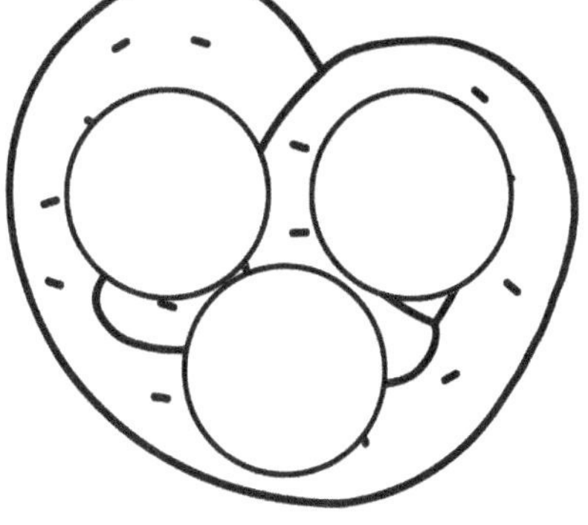

Counting

Count the items and write the number below

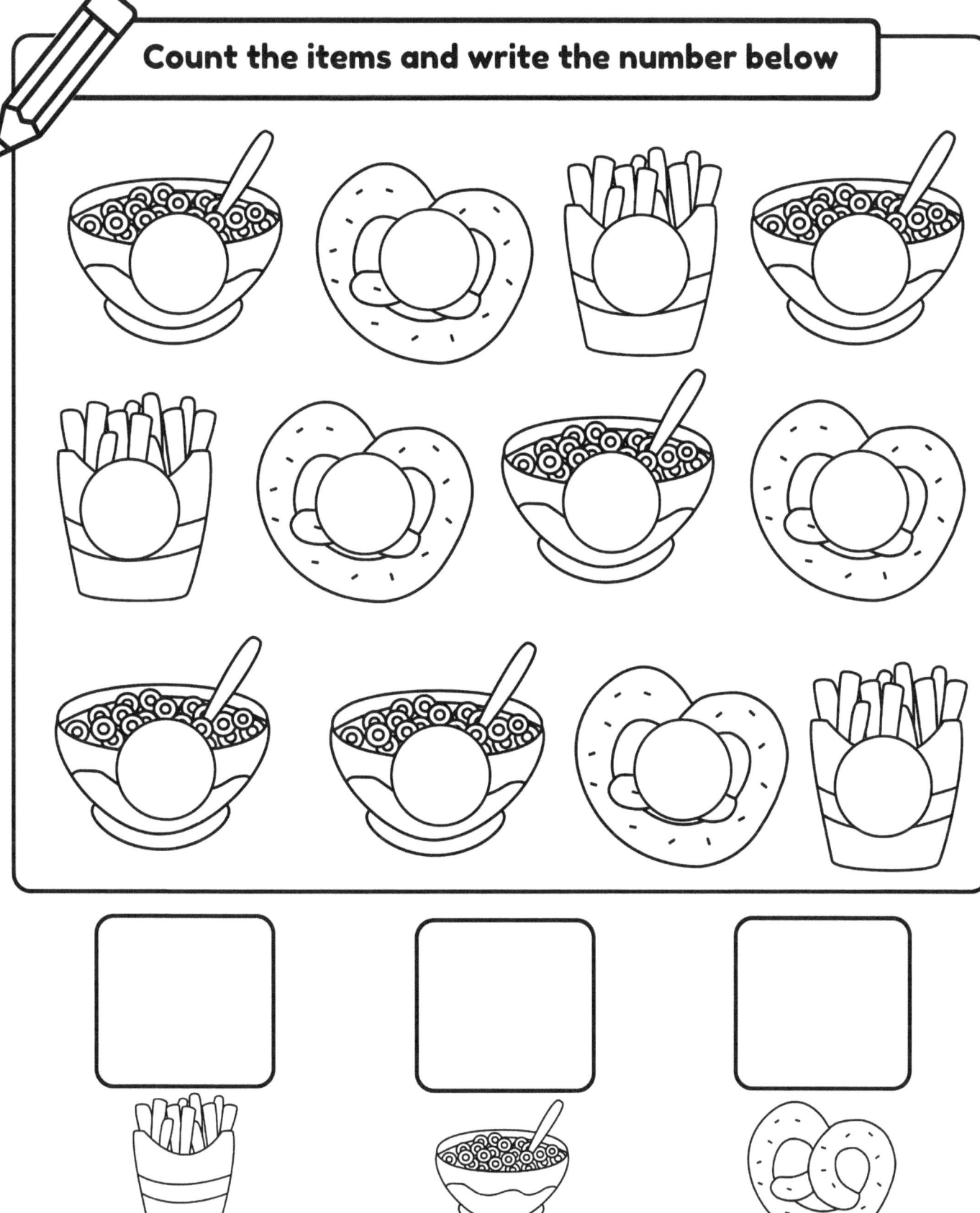

Week 11

Find the Shadow

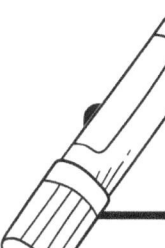

Dot the circle to find the shadow

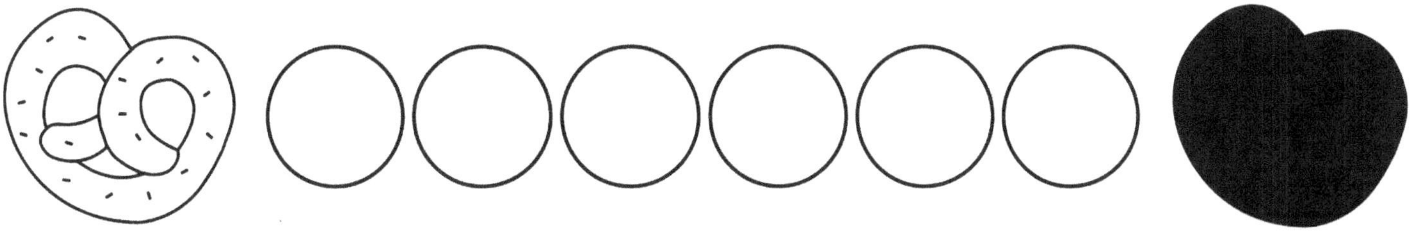

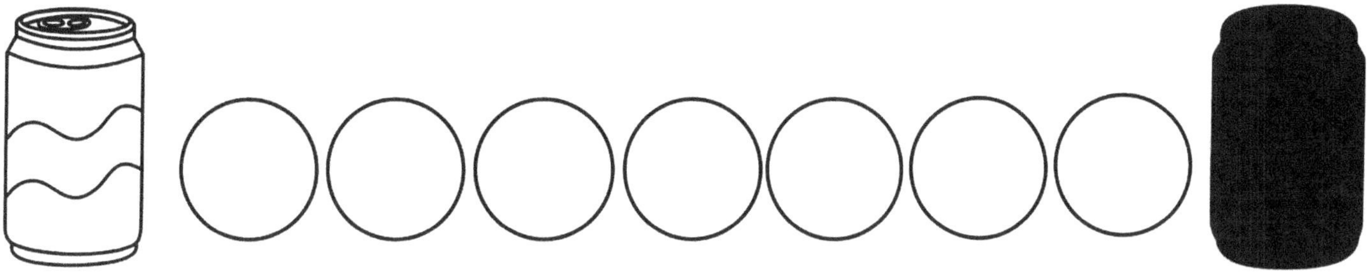

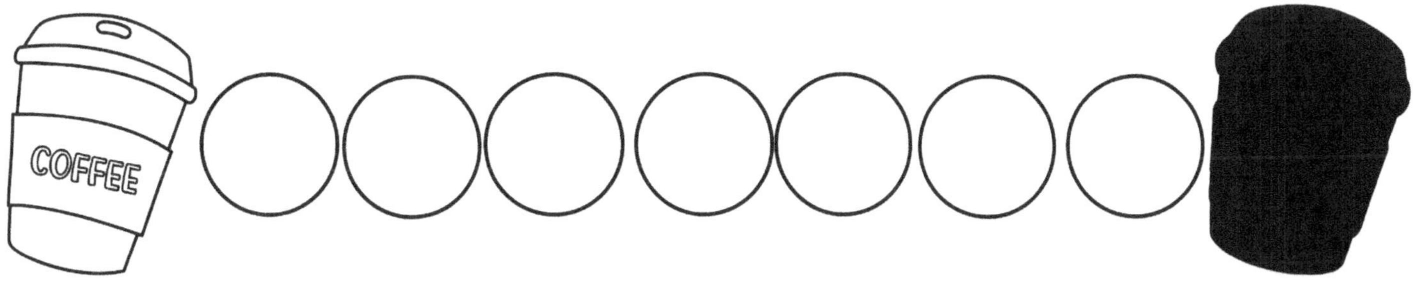

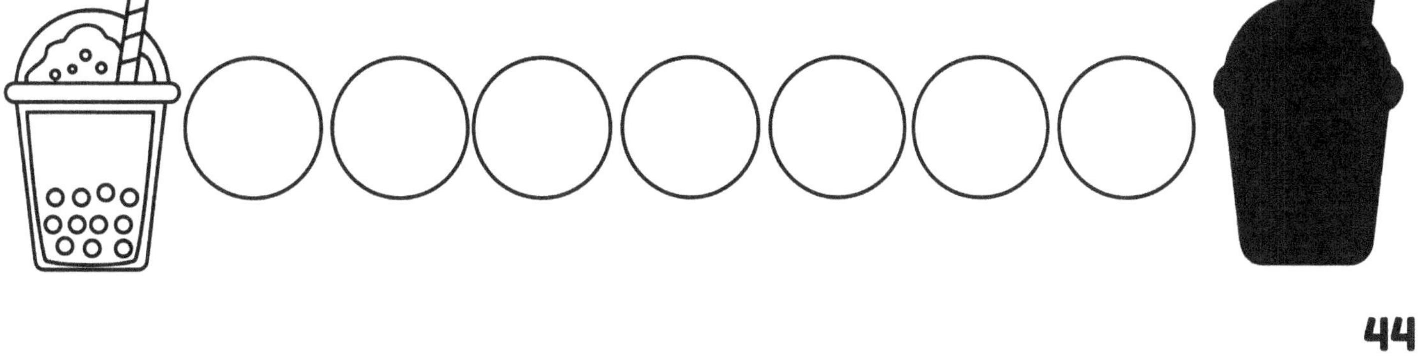

Milkshake

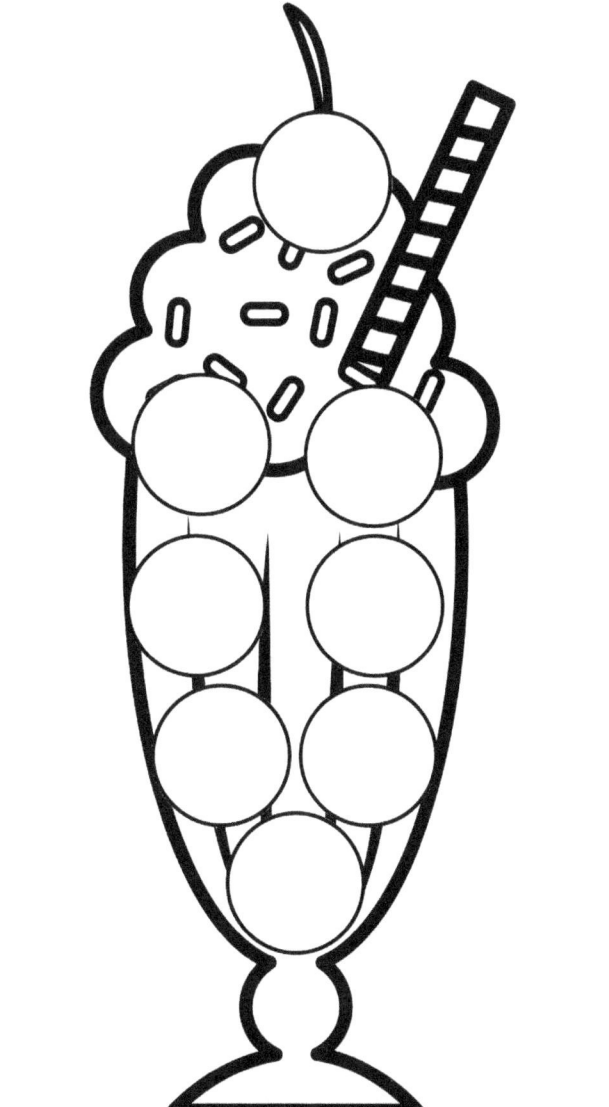

Spell out "Milkshake" by dotting each letter

M   i   l   k   -

s   h   a   k   e

Week 12

Scissor Practice

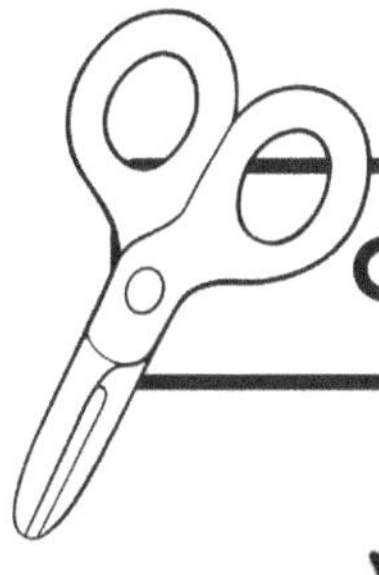

Cut along the dotted line to practice your scissor skills.

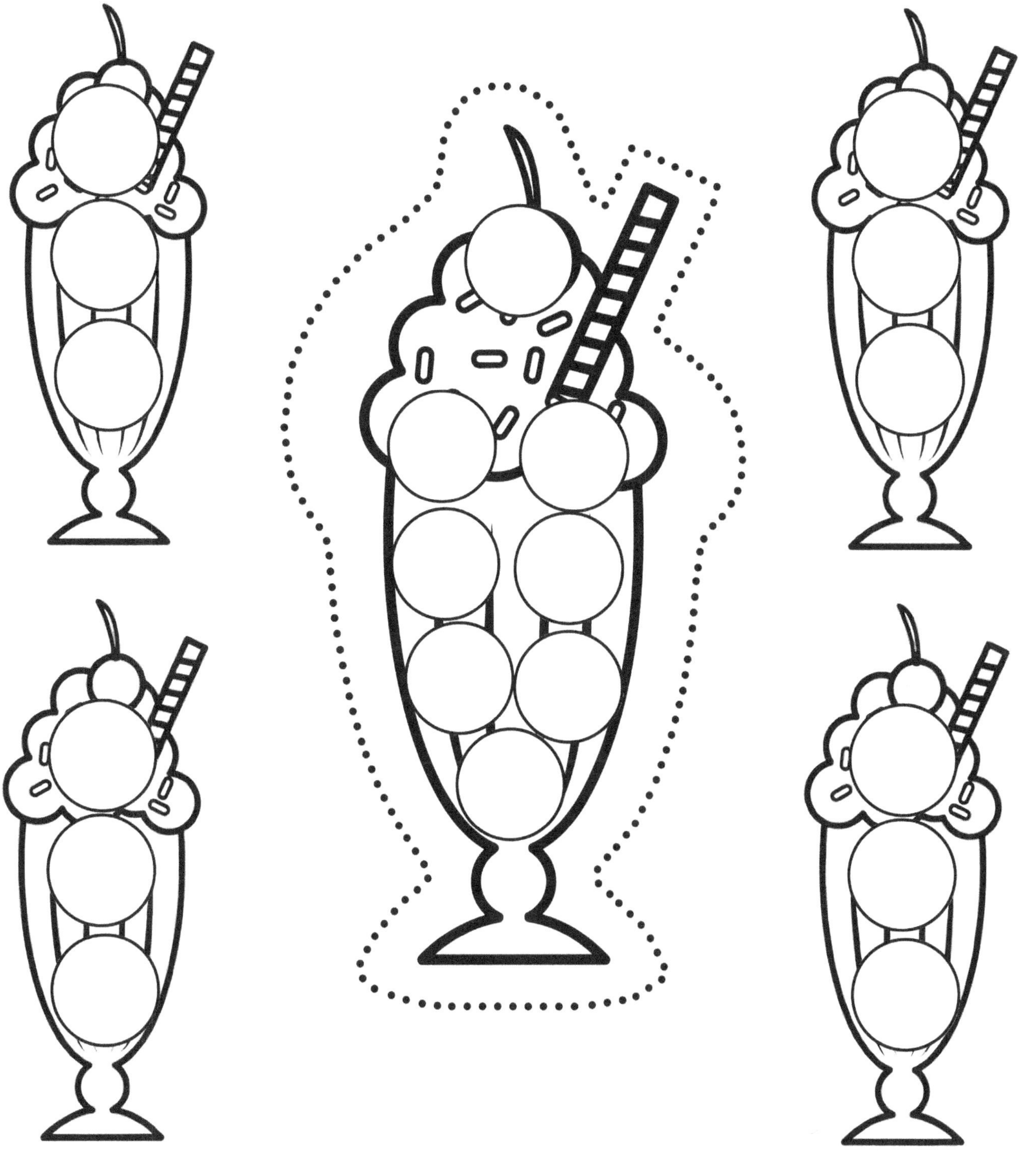

I Spy

Find the Milkshake and dot it.

Maze

Dot the circles to help Jolina find the milkshake.

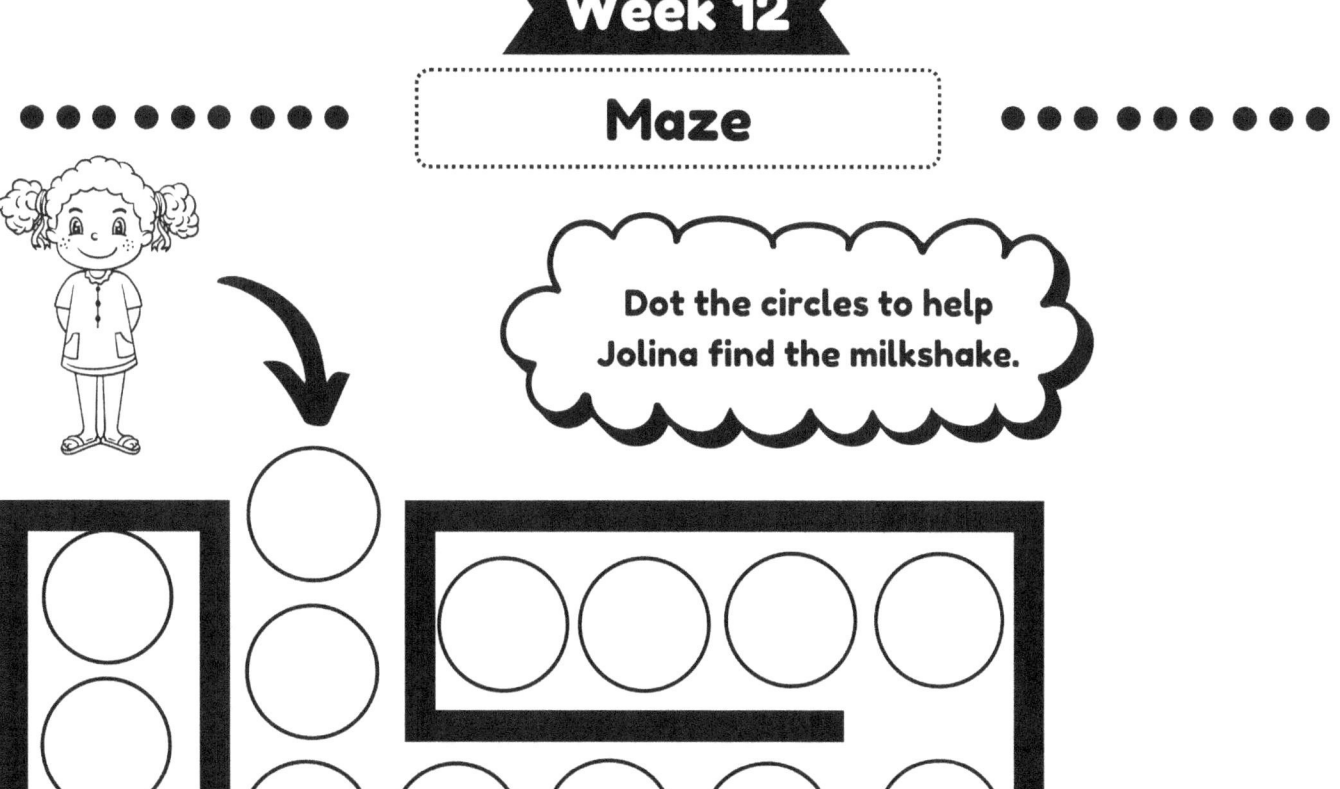

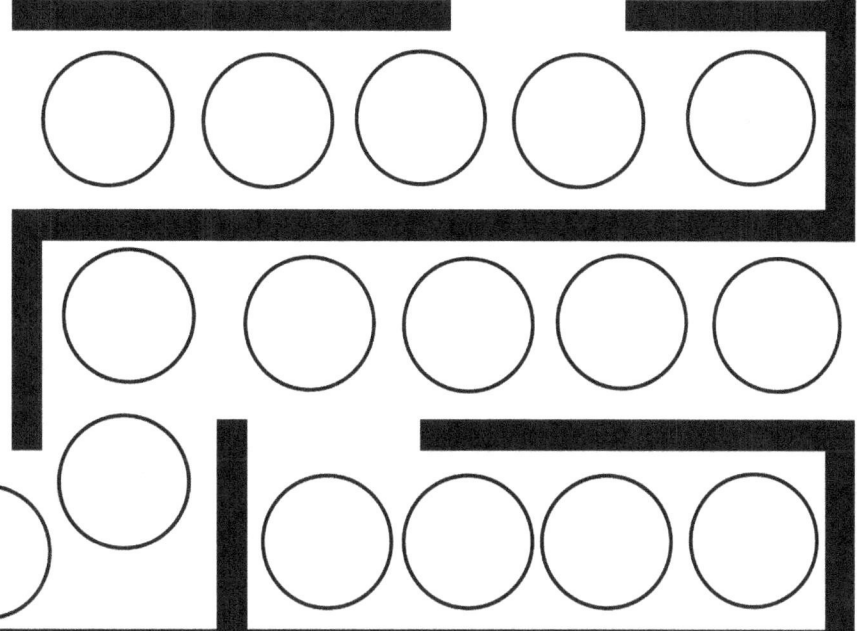

Great Job!
Jolina found the milkshake!

Pizza

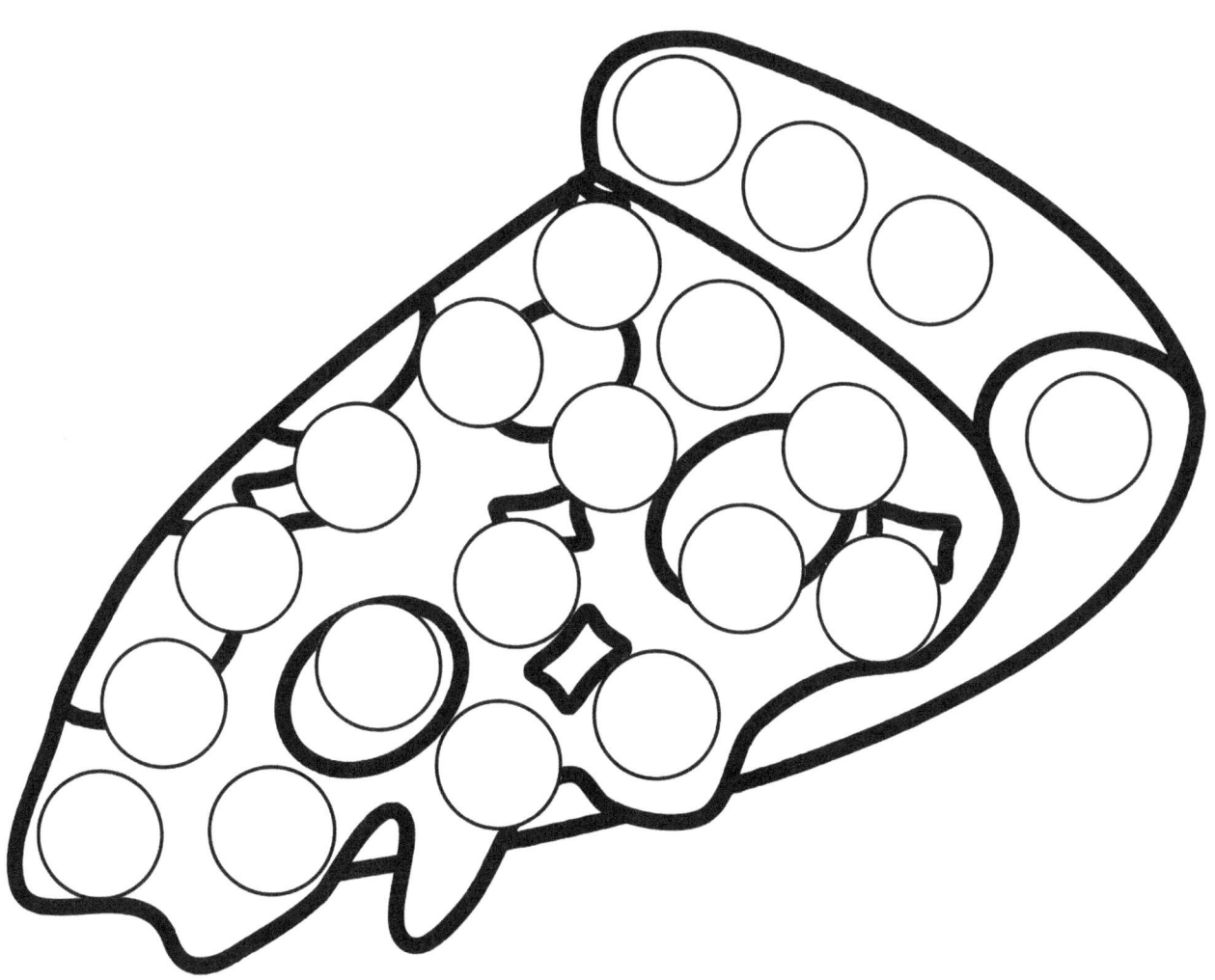

Spell out "Pizza" by dotting each letter

P   i   z   z   a

Week 13

Scissor Practice

Cut along the dotted line to practice your scissor skills.

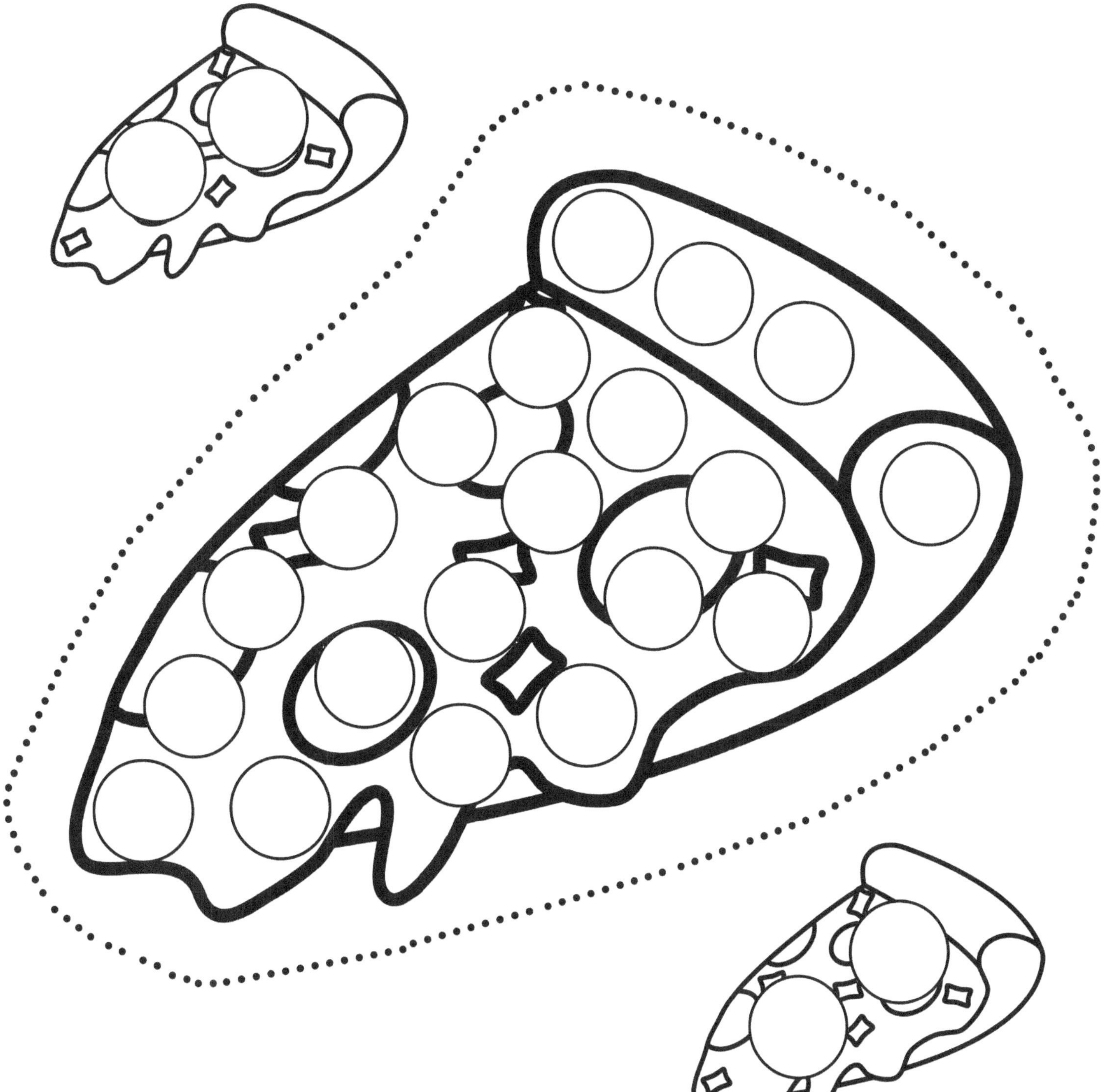

Counting

Count the items and write the number below

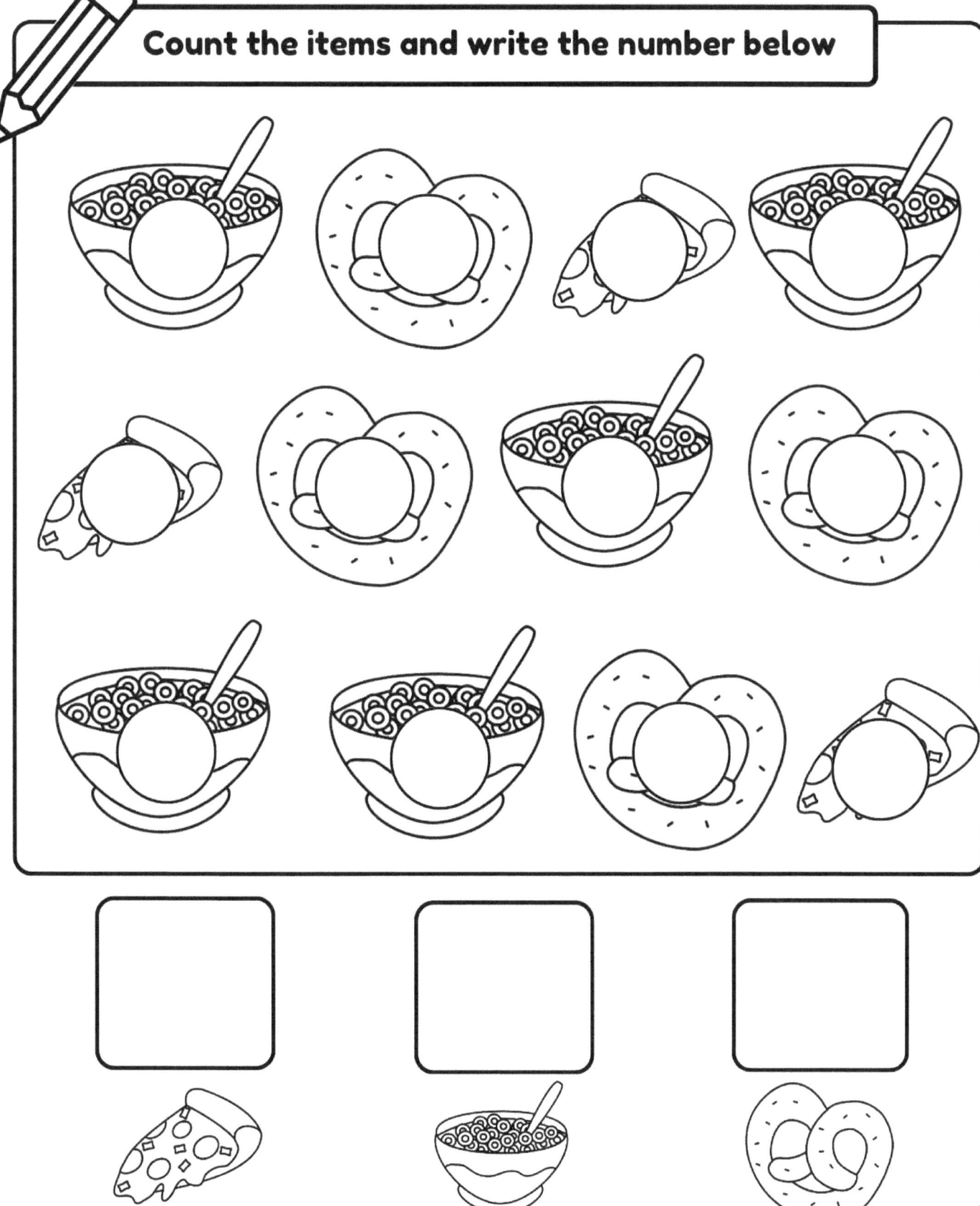

Find the Shadow

Dot the circle to find the shadow

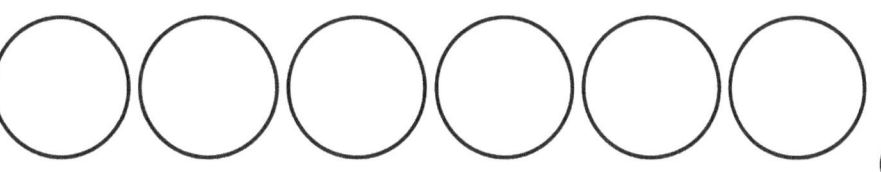

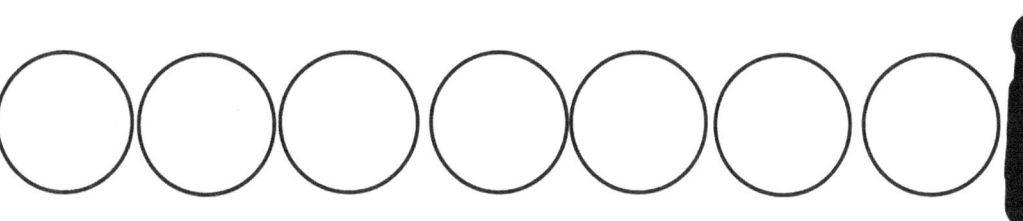

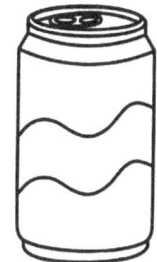
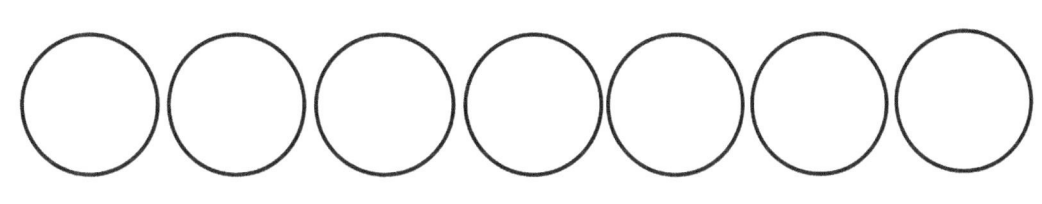

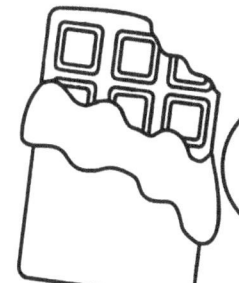
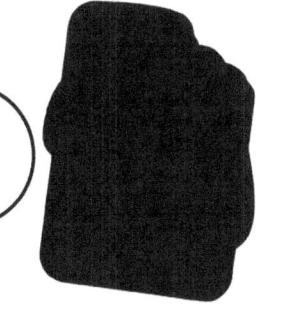

Free Printable Activity Book!

- **Ignites Imagination:** Coloring with a story helps kids picture scenes and boost creativity.
- **Boosts Reading:** Following the story while coloring improves reading skills naturally.
- **Enhances Focus:** Storytelling with coloring keeps kids engaged and builds concentration.
- **Fosters Connection:** Coloring helps kids emotionally bond with characters and plots.
- **Fun Learning:** Makes learning enjoyable and easy through playful coloring.

Parents & Teachers!

Our biggest joy comes from helping little ones flourish and discover the world around them through learning.

That's why your thoughts matter so much to us!

Your honest thoughts about our book, even a quick sentence or two, would mean the world. We really mean it!

You'd be making a big difference for a small education brand like ours, run with love by a mother-daughter team.

Your reviews help us reach more curious minds across the globe, paving their way to success in their educational journey.

And hey, maybe we'll even sell a few more books in the process!

Every single review makes our hearts swell with gratitude.

Ready to make our day?

Scan the QR Code below to share your thoughts.

www.ingramcontent.com/pod-product-compliance
Lightning Source LLC
Chambersburg PA
CBHW081004120626
46546CB00010B/3008